Seven First Words of Jesus

SEVEN FIRST WORDS OF JESUS

J. Winston Pearce

BROADMAN PRESS
Nashville, Tennessee

Dewey Decimal Classification: 232.95
Library of Congress catalog card number: 66–10668
Printed in the United States of America
5.Te.65 KSP

To
My cherished friends
of the
First Baptist Church,
Durham, North Carolina
who were
partners with me in the gospel
for
fourteen significant years

Preface

The material in this book is based upon seven of the recorded first words of Jesus. We do not know what *the* seven first words of Jesus were. There may be real difference of opinion as to which are the seven *first recorded* words. There is no question but that the seven first words used in these chapters are among the first recorded words.

The messages represent an effort to look carefully at the beginning of the earthly ministry of Jesus, to see the factors, the influences, and the convictions that shaped the "Galilean Sunshine" and its significance.

Grace Noll Crowell has a little poem in which is voiced the prayer, "God, keep a clean wind blowing through my heart." May the same "clean wind" that blew through the minds and hearts of those who first heard these early words of the Master blow through our lives as we reverently hear the words again.

Contents

Introduction

Robert Louis Stevenson once wrote his friend, William Ernest Henley, a delightful letter claiming that he had discovered a number of hitherto unknown works by great masters. He said that the find included a novel by Fielding, a half-dozen tragedies by Shakespeare, parts of a journal kept by the bard, as well as an unfinished biography. Stevenson describes his own fever of excitement over the imagined discovery.

Stevenson's flight of imagination is not so farfetched. Hitherto undiscovered manuscripts are frequently coming to light. The most exciting of these have been, and continue to be, in the realm of biblical manuscripts. What if one day we came upon a well-preserved scroll giving us accurate, authentic, and detailed information about "the hidden years" of Jesus? Imagine finding such a document written by a boyhood friend of Jesus, one who had played games with him in the streets of Nazareth, one who had gone fishing with him, one who had been a fellow student in the local synagogue with him, one who had observed his skills in the carpenter shop and noted his love for children.

Luke wrote: "Inasmuch as many have undertaken to compile a narrative of the things which have been accomplished

11

among us . . . it seemed good to me also, having followed all things closely for some time past, to write an orderly account for you" (1:1-3, RSV). Later in Acts he wrote: "In the first book, O Theophilus, I have dealt with all that Jesus began to do and teach, until the day when he was taken up."

Yet, in spite of Luke's carefulness in "having followed all things closely," in spite of his "orderly account," for which we are profoundly grateful, the fact remains that we are faced with "the hidden years" of Jesus. Only one peep at the page which lets us see him—as Milton puts it, "Ere yet my age had measured twice six years"—then the book closes and silence reigns.

It is not total silence. The skilled biographer makes two approaches when faced with a silence in the life of his subject. First, he may reconstruct a picture of the times in which his character lived; he studies the habits and customs of the people; he observes the pattern of households, schools, churches, business, games, the economy, and the laws of the land. The careful biographer then tries to place his subject in such an environment. Second, the biographer studies all the writings and pronouncements of his character in later life to see if these might throw light upon that dark period.

Both these veins of ore have been worked diligently in seeking to reveal the hidden years of Jesus. We probably know more about the land, the people, the laws, the customs, the traditions, the memories, the dreams and the hopes, the homes and public institutions of Palestine during those silent years of Jesus than of any similar period in the history of the world. Skilled and brilliant minds, warm and devoted hearts, amply financed hands have done their work well. Libraries have been pored over, caves have been searched, excavations have been made, sands have been sifted, inscriptions have been deciphered. This same kind of attention has been given

also to the teachings of Jesus. The learnings of the centuries
have been laid lovingly along side his words. No reported
word of his has failed to receive all but unbelievable scru-
tiny.

Devout scholars believe that through these two channels
they have been able to reconstruct a reliable picture. Many
of the metaphors we find in the teachings of Jesus were
probably drawn directly from his home life during those
silent years. Scholars believe that Jesus noted his mother
patching the little garments for his brothers and sisters; that
he saw her place yeast in the flour and then watched it "leaven
the whole lump." He was probably sent to the market to buy
"two sparrows for a farthing." Outside Nazareth he observed
the "fields that are white unto harvest" and "the lilies of the
field" that outdid Solomon's splendor. He must have seen
children sulking at play, refusing either to dance at the mock
wedding or to mourn at the simulated funeral. He heard of a
woman who pestered the judge until he "avenged her
wrong." He knew of wayward sons who begged for "the
portion of goods" that was theirs and then wasted it all in
riotous living. From Joseph, his foster father, he learned that
no father would ever give his son stones for bread or serpents
in the place of fish.

Thomas Carlyle and Ralph Waldo Emerson left notebooks
and journals written early in life containing notes, jottings,
ideas, and allusions which later grew into sharp and meaty
discussions. Even so, the early experiences of Jesus made their
contribution to his later teaching and preaching.

Arthur John Gossip believed that the action of Mary, his
mother, at the wedding in Cana gives us valuable insight. You
recall that the wine ran out. Mary observed the whispering
among the servants, heard from them of the difficulty, and
then did a revealing thing. She knew there was one present

who could always be depended upon to meet any emergency; she had never known him to be indifferent; he always managed to find a way. So, no matter how the response of Jesus sounds to us, Mary spoke to the servants with confidence in words like these: "Do not worry. Jesus knows about it. Whatever he tells you to do, do it. I do not know how he will deal with the situation, but I know he will; he always does."

In *The Jesus of History*, T. R. Glover suggests that the phrase we so often use in hymns, poetry, and sermons, "Come to Jesus," may have started in a very natural and spontaneous way in the home and carpenter shop. When the children would be cross and fretful, when Mary had heavy chores, the words would sound, "Come to Jesus." Then into the carpenter shop, or out into the fields, he would take the children where his loving acceptance, keen interest, and wise initiative would turn boredom into adventure and irritation into excitement.

When scholars and artists have done their work conscientiously and well, drawing upon their sure knowledge of the times and a careful study of the later teachings of Jesus, there still remains one and only one recorded incident in the early life of Jesus. Therefore, this event and the words of Jesus recorded there are deeply significant. And his early commitment, his struggle against worldly goals, and the men he chose to be with him during the thousand days of his earthly ministry are the concerns of this book.

1

"My Father's Business"

LUKE 2:40–50

What is the significance of this single recorded event in the "silent years" of Jesus? Significant it must be, else why would it alone have been preserved?

> What was he doing all that time
> From boyhood then to early prime,
> Was he then idle, or the less,
> About his Father's business? [1]

The answer to the first question has to be, "We do not know." The answer to the last two questions are, "No." He was not idle, neither was he less about his Father's business. There are definite indications of these answers in the recorded event of the twelve-year-old Jesus.

The incident indicates a danger that is inherent in being a disciple of Jesus. We may lose him; his parents did. To be sure, in a real sense one can never lose God. He is "everywhere present for good." If we ascend into heaven he is there; if we make our beds in hell he is there; if we dwell in the uttermost parts of the earth, his hand will lead and his right hand hold. In another sense, however, one may lose the Christ.

We lose him by not giving first attention to his major
interests. When the mother of Jesus remonstrated that she
and Joseph had sought for him, he seemed surprised and said
they should have known where to find him. They should
have known that his chief interest was the house and business
of God. They found him when they came where men were
concerned about the Scriptures, about the word, way, and
will of God.

God is concerned with more than just the churches and
what goes on in them. Indeed, he may be more concerned
with what goes on at the plant, factory, and office than he is
with what goes on at church. If this is the case, it is because
more of his children are in plants, factories, and offices than
are in his churches. This does not gainsay the fact men have
found Christ in the churches. They have found him when
they gave themselves to a serious consideration of Scriptures;
when they have gone with their fellows to the house of God
and engaged in prayer; when they have seriously sought the
way and will of God through the experiences of worship.

Lines of   If you are to find Christ
Prayer   "where cross the crowded
ways of life," you must first
learn to recognize him in the place where cross the lines of
prayer. If God is to be recognized on the Plains of Bethel, he
must first be seen on the ladder that reaches from earth to
heaven: first the perpendicular, then the horizontal. The
heavens must open before earth is seen as the house of God.
First comes the fatherhood of God; after that you may experience the true brotherhood of man. The only way you can
understand that you and another are brothers is to admit that
you have the same Father.

We are hearing much criticism today of the local church.

No informed man can deny that much of the criticism is justified. As Walter Rauschenbusch said long ago, "When we judge her by the mind of her Master, we bow in pity and contrition." But we need also to join Rauschenbusch when he says, "When we compare her with all other human institutions, we rejoice, for there is none like her." Let not the impatient and rebellious forget that! Let the critic be slow in his wholesale condemnation of the church. Men and women, youth, boys and girls still find Christ in the community of faith. They find him there, and then with Christ they go into the Nazareths of business, labor, politics, recreation, education, and home.

We lose Christ by being preoccupied with, excessively involved in, the petty cares and joys of everyday existence. It is very easy to make out a strong case for this sort of concern. You may feel that just because you are concerned with the *here* and *now*, you deserve some sort of merit badge. Jesus did come "eating and drinking"; he was one with his brethren; he did bear the sins of many; he did not isolate himself from the present conditions of men. His followers, too, must walk, sit, talk, and serve as their Master did; if they do not do so, they will lose him.

Let his followers remember, however, why he went among his brethren; and, let his followers not forget what he went among his brethren to accomplish. He went because he was sent by God to bring them back to God. He entered into the joys and sorrows of his brethren to sanctify that which was good, to rebuke and to forgive that which was bad, and never to lose himself just to satisfy his physical needs.

When Columbus returned to Spain after having discovered America, the Spaniards demanded proof of his discovery. How did they know that he had discovered a new world? He gave them numerous proofs; he showed them strange and different plants and products. The explorer's crowning proof, however, was a new and different man. He showed them an Indian. Then the Spaniards believed that he had discovered a new world. This is the reason for becoming involved with the "world," whether it be a new world or an old world; it is that new men may come forth. This never takes place when we lose Christ through preoccupation with the petty cares and joys of daily existence rather than giving ourselves to the "great affairs of life."

Independence Granted and Guided We learn that the twelve-year-old Jesus was given a degree of independence, and that he accepted and used it. We may wonder how the parents could go a full day's journey without knowing that Jesus was not in the party. However, the women probably traveled in a group to themselves, and they may have left early because they traveled more slowly. The men would travel in a group to themselves, and the children might be in either group. Mary may have thought that Jesus was traveling with Joseph; Joseph supposed that the lad had gone on ahead with his mother. They both felt no hesitation in leaving him to make his own decisions. They knew that he was reliable. They trusted him; he knew that they trusted him; he gave a worthy response to their trust.

The modern parent often feels frustrated in the area of child teaching and training. Just what is required? What does the parent owe the child? What can the parent do that will best prepare the child for the difficult world into which he goes, for decisions he will have to make, for adjustment to the society and culture of which the child must become a part? The parent can neither hold on to the child, making his decisions for him, nor make a place for him throughout life.

At the same time, it is not enough to "have them and leave them" as we are sometimes advised. Even the beasts of the forest do better than that.

One of the great needs is for the child to be successfully guided into independence. Wise are the parents who are able to give the child the sense of independence and, at the same time, love and guidance. If the child can feel that he is not only being allowed to make his own decisions but is expected to make them; if the child knows that he is expected to make these decisions at each stage of his development, yet makes them within the context of the love, interest, and concern of the parents; if the child knows that the parent is always available to him for whatever help may be needed; then the child can feel secure and yet develop a healthy independence.

In writing about his mother, Ramsay MacDonald said that she thought of her children as treasures given to her to guard and protect but not to mold in her own image. He said that she knew the child was an individual and not an appendage; she felt that it was her duty to enrich the life of the child by teaching him how to use his own talents. She felt that it was her responsibility to provide him with an atmosphere in which to breathe, a purity for him to feel, and a liberty for him to employ. He felt that she was saying to the children, "I am at hand to hold and to help you *if necessary,* but I want you to develop your own little selves so that when you are men and women you will be persons of a free will and not creatures of circumstance." [2]

While fully acknowledging the divinity in Jesus, one may still ask whether the influence of the home in Nazareth, an influence that respected the child as an individual person and assumed that he would act responsibly, did not reveal itself later in the attitude of Jesus toward persons. One person who had carefully read the Gospels straight through was asked what was the dominant impression that he gained; he answered, "The impression that Jesus never met an unimportant person."

A delightful incident in the life of the great Chief Justice Oliver Wendell Holmes speaks to this truth. One day while walking, he was joined by a little girl. They walked and talked together for a bit, and then the little girl announced that she had to go home. Justice Holmes suggested that if her mother asked her where she had been, the child might say she had been walking with Oliver Wendell Holmes. To this the child replied, "And when your folk ask you where you have been, tell them that you have been walking with Mary Susan Brown."

Awakening   This Temple incident in
Interest   the boyhood of Jesus also
                       shows us his awakening interests. Nazareth was a small town; Jerusalem was a great city. What would you expect to capture the interest of a twelve-year-old boy from a small town visiting a great city for the first time? Transfer the scene to a modern metropolis. If a boy were missing, would the parents look for him at the zoo, at the firehouse with its trucks and ladders, at the railroad station with its locomotives, among the canyons of tall buildings, or in the museum?

It is easy to magnify the Temple experience out of the proportion that the Spirit of God probably meant us to understand it. Everything about the scene would indicate that Jesus was in most ways a normal boy. The remonstrance of his mother, the boy's reply, his return to Nazareth and his obedience, the record of his growth in wisdom, size, and favor with God and man—all these indicate a normal home and boyhood. But his *interest* was different from what we expect a normal boy of twelve to have. Instead of the usual places a twelve-year-old boy might have been, *this* boy was found in church; he was with ministers and "professional" religious people.

When a modern mother exerted great effort to make her way through the crowd in order that her son might shake hands with a great man, the boy extended his left hand. "Why do you not give me your right hand?" asked the distinguished guest. "Can't," replied the boy. "I've got my marbles in it." Marbles instead of greatness. We are not surprised at that; for that boy marbles were more important. But not the boy of whom we now speak.

That says a great deal about the interests of the twelve-year-old Jesus. It also says something about those mature men in the Temple, and what it says is good. They had time for the boy. They listened to his questions; they answered his questions. When they asked him questions, they listened to his answers. President Garfield was once asked, "Why do you bow to that newsboy? "Because," answered the President, "no one knows what is buttoned up in that boy's jacket." I am glad that mature men listened to young Jesus that day.

Again, in this incident we are allowed to see a dawning conviction. He said, "Did you not know that I must be in my Father's house?" or "about my Father's business?" Books have been written, arguments have been staged in an effort to decide just when and where and under what conditions Jesus became aware of his unique relationship with his Heavenly Father. We cannot give a conclusive answer to that question, but we can know the answer made by Jesus. Was it a gentle but firm reminder to Mary, as well as to all and each, that God was his Father, his Father in a unique way, a way that he was not the Father of any other boy? We may not be

dogmatic, but somewhere Jesus had to become conscious of
his special relationship. It surely was not in the manger on the
night when the shepherds came and the angels sang nor when
the Wise Men offered their gifts of gold, frankincense, and
myrrh. It may be that here in the Temple the truth became
more clear than it had ever been before, that here he discovered who he was. Perhaps something that the teachers said in
answer to some youthful but probing question that the boy
asked led him to know that he was God's Son as other sons
were not. And could it be that this is why we have the curtain
of light raised on those hidden years just at this spot and for
this particular time?

"Father" was his chosen word for God. Over and over again
he used the word. He used it when he prayed; he used it when
he taught and preached; he used it in joy, in grief, in life, and
in death. "Holy Father," "Righteous Father," "Father, I
thank thee," "Father who art in heaven," "Father, keep them
in thy name," "Father, I will that they shall be with me,"
"In my Father's house," "It is not your Father's will,"
"Father, if it be possible," "Father, forgive them," "Father,
into thy hands"—these are just a few times when Jesus used
the word. Did he use it first with dawning significance in the
Temple when he was twelve? Incidentally, what a compliment to Joseph is the use that Jesus made of the word,
"Father"!

Glad   Look further and see how
Surrender   this incident emphasizes sur-
                            render. His words were, "I
must be in my Father's house." Here is the imperative of
surrender in the incident of the first recorded word of Jesus.
We dislike these words; we often rebel at their implication.
There is implied force, either outward or inward. There is

the note of discipline in the words, learned from within or enforced from without. They do not sound like freedom and liberty, and these are words we do like. We respond vigorously to Robert Frost's line, "Something there is that does not like a wall." We may be like Chiara, a character in *The Shoes of the Fisherman*. "She was not wholly free, nor wholly loved, nor wholly protected, but she had enough of each to make life bearable." [3] We want our freedom, and we do not want the word "must" to direct our lives.

"I must be in my Father's house" or "about my Father's business." Who said he did? Who was forcing him to that? What kind of legal code was "putting the screws" on him? Love, duty, service, sacrifice, salvation were a few of the "taskmasters" of his life whispering their imperial "musts" in the ear of his soul!

It was love that whispered, "I must be in my Father's house." It was duty that affirmed, "I must be about my Father's business." It was purpose that rang out, "I must work the works of him who sent me while it is day." It was compassion that sounded in the words, "He must needs go through Samaria." It was the voice of sacrifice that affirmed: "The Son of man must be lifted up." It was the peal of victory that shouted, "The third day the Son of man must rise again." This imperial "must" is used no less than thirty times in the New Testament in relation to Jesus and his mission.

It is reported that once when the present Queen Elizabeth was a small child, she became angry, stamped her foot, and shouted, "I am a princess, and so I can do whatever I want to do!" Her father, the king, replied gently but firmly and a bit sadly, "No, my dear. It is just because you are a princess that you cannot do as you please." It is a true observation. The greater one is, the more "musts" there are in his life.

It is easy to become confused about words. We dislike the

word "must"; we like the word "freedom." But what if it is
only through "must" that one arrives at "freedom"? In athlet-
ics this is true. The young woman who wins an Olympic gold
medal for swimming has great freedom, but she arrived at it
only through many "musts" of discipline and training. It is
true in music; the Paganinis who thrill the world with their
violins know freedom, but it is only because they obeyed the
great "musts" of discipline and practice through the years.
The same is true of farming and medicine and selling. It is
easy to become envious of the saints. We see them striding
through spiritual difficulties with a mastery that all but
overwhelms us. It was not always so. Read their biographies,
and you will find that the heights of these great men were not
attained by sudden flight; they conquered through the peril,
toil, and pain of "must."

The Chicago Temple is a Methodist church in the heart of
the Windy City's commercial and financial district. Often in
walking through the "Loop," I have looked up, up, up at the
church's steeple. There atop the tall steeple is a cross, said to
be the highest cross in the world. Charles M. Crowe tells of a
traffic jam that occurred at the base of the building some
years ago. Thousands of people had stopped and were gazing
upward to that cross. Why? It had been there many years;
most people gave it only an occasional glance. Now it was
stopping traffic. The difference? A man was on it. A workman
was repairing the cross, and Chicago stopped to see. "Even so
must the Son of man be lifted up." "And I, if I be lifted
up . . . will draw all men unto me."

Look again. Jesus in the Temple when he was twelve tells
us also about obedience. After that experience "he went
down with them and came to Nazareth, and was obedient to
them." The dawning consciousness of his unique relationship
to God, his clear understanding of the imperial call of duty,

the "musts" of life—these did not keep him from obedience in the home. His great experiences in the Temple and his high discoveries there did not make him proud. He was no less an earthly son because he had a divine Father. The fact that he heard heaven's imperative did not mean that he would ignore earthly commands. The fact that he had to be about his Father's business did not mean that he could neglect the business of Joseph and the carpenter shop. He apparently saw no conflict between the work of God and the work of man. He came down and was obedient unto his parents and to the work that needed to be done in order that the needs of men might be met, and that his parents, his little brothers and sisters might be fed, clothed, and sheltered.

Playing God Some years ago a tourist visited Anton Lang's pottery shop in Oberammergau. For many years, Lang had played the part of Christ in the famous Passion Play at Oberammergau; probably no other man has been as well known for playing this part. He had received the plaudits of the world. Now too feeble to carry the heavy cross of the Christus upon his shoulders, the old man was making objects with his hands in a humble pottery shop. The visitor expressed his sympathy and his regret that the great artist had found it necessary to retire from acting the part of Christ in the Passion Play. Then Anton Lang spoke a word that should be remembered. Said he, "I still feel I'm playing God if I shape things well." I do not know what the heavenly choir was singing at that moment, but I wonder if there was not suddenly a great silence as God said, "Well done, for the servant has claimed sonship!"

Years later when Jesus stood waist deep in the Jordan and was baptized by John, there came a voice from heaven saying,

"This is my beloved Son, in whom I am well pleased." Look at that sentence, "My beloved Son, in whom I am well pleased." Jesus had not yet preached a sermon; he had not performed a miracle; he had not instructed a disciple. But his Father said, "In him I am well pleased."

> Very dear the Cross of Shame
> Where he took the sinner's blame,
>   And the tomb wherein he lay
> Until the third day came.
> But he walked the self-same road,
> And he bore the self-same load,
>   When the Carpenter of Nazareth,
> Made common things for God.[4]

"Our Lord must have put much of His service of God and of His love to Him," says Gossip, "into the thoroughness with which He sawed and planed and laboured at His ordinary humdrum daily task. Justin Martyr tells us that in his day there were still implements in existence said to have come from Christ's own hands. One can be sure that His whole heart had been put into the making of them, that to every customer He gave His very best, as He stood there among the clean, sweet-smelling shavings, working at cradles and at coffins, those symbols of the mysteries and depth of life, and at the little homely things no less. Well may the Moravians pray in their litany, 'May the precious sweat of Thy labour lighten our toil,' and again, 'May Thy faithfulness in Thy handicraft make us faithful in our share of labour.' "[5]

How this truth does need to be emphasized today! We have often been reminded that although Jesus was a carpenter, the churches have pretty well lost the working men as a group. There are other groups that the churches have lost to be sure. We have pretty well lost educators as a group; we have fairly well lost the scientists, the entertainers, and others as groups. Yet, there seems to be something especially disturbing about losing the working man, since God's Son was one of them. Since he did nothing to leave them out, his followers must bear the blame.

We may feel that there is little similarity in the work that a skilled artisan does in a great factory today, whether furniture or automobile, and the work that was done in the carpenter's shop at Nazareth. It is true. Still, if the product is a needed product, if the work is done honestly, if a man pours his heart as well as his talents into it, if the work is done for the good of man and the glory of God, a man may say with Anton Lang, "I still feel I'm playing God if I shape things well."

Ruskin was once admiring one of the great old cathedrals and was given permission to climb into its heights to make a close observation of the quality of its workmanship. There he was delighted to find on the capitals, lost in the height, where it was never expected that human eye would see, in dark and dust of the centuries, that the traceries, the decorative inter- lacing of lines, were as beautifully, delicately, and carefully done as were those that stood in the full floodlight of the worshiping congregation!

Our day has much for which to repent; surely high on its list is our downgrading of the place of the honest working man, our placing of the "professional" near the top of the ladder and the laboring man on the bottom rung. We place the industrialist and merchant on the pedestal and usually consign to the basement of our concern and economy the men and women of the night shifts and the migrant workers. It was different in the Middle Ages. The clergy was placed at the top, the nobility was just below the clergy, the serfs and artisans were next, and last—the very last—was the merchant and businessman. This was no better than what we do; it was

only reversing the order. The ground before the grace of God is level for all men and all honest work. As Browning said, "There is no least nor first."

So, while we wish that the curtain might have been lifted more often on those hidden years of Jesus we may be exceedingly grateful for the single incident that was revealed. We may wish that we might know more about that event, but until we are willing to profit more from that fleeting glimpse, we have no valid reason for complaining about what we do not have. It has been said that if one-tenth of the things we say we believe as Christians are really true, then we ought to be at least ten times as enthusiastic as we are. 'Tis only a brief lifting of the curtain, but if we really believe what we have seen from that lifting, it will make all the difference that is necessary! For here are convictions: convictions about self, about God, about human relations, about work, about God's work and God's house—and God's everlasting "must" is laid across the top of each!

2
"We Do Well to Conform"
MATTHEW 3:13–17; MARK 1:9–11; LUKE 3:21–22

The hour had struck for Jesus. For thirty years he had been biding his time. For most of these thirty years, he had been "making things for God" in the carpenter shop at Nazareth; both he and his work had been pleasing to God, for it was his Father's business that he was doing. But now the summons was to a new and different task. As Francis Thompson said, there came a trumpet sound "from the hid battlements of Eternity." The Trumpeter he knew, and he knew what the trumpet said. How did the call come to him? What was the setting for it? What means, human or otherwise, did God use? What were its distinctive notes—notes that called for and received the full and complete commitment of Jesus?

The call came in connection with the preaching of a great man, John the Baptist. Crowds from Jerusalem had come to the Jordan as to a revival meeting. Many who "came to scoff, remained to pray." It was a scene of mass evangelism with no holds barred! There was much of the "hellfire and damnation" in the message that was preached. But the people heard, and the people heeded, for John was a *man*. No one who saw him, heard him, felt his influence, and observed his habits could doubt that. He was a man, but he was more: he was a *man of God.* Thomas Carlyle once said of a certain church and people that what was needed was a preacher who knew God other than secondhand. John was such a preacher. His hearers knew it. There had been no such preaching in Israel since the days of the great prophets. A man of God had come with *God's message.* John cared only for two things, his Master and his message. He was not concerned about personal preferment; he was content to decrease so long as his Master increased. No wonder the people heard, heeded, and were healed!

A Great   To this outdoor revival on
Encounter   the banks of the Jordan Jesus
                     came and presented himself
for baptism. John demurred; Jesus insisted; John baptized him. It was a strange scene. The incident not only troubled John, it has troubled Christians ever since! John felt that it was he who should be baptized by Jesus and not the other way around. And were it not for our assurance of the superior wisdom of Jesus, we would most certainly vote with John. As we see it, there were several things that Jesus might have done. Any one of these things might be easier for us to understand than what Jesus actually did do.

He might have ignored the whole situation. Baptism, as such, was not new. The mystery religions practiced it; their initiations were largely based upon baptism. The Jews practiced baptism for proselytes as they came into the Jewish faith from paganism. This was to be expected for these proselytes had to be purged from the evil of their Gentile ways. But for someone to say that a Jew, a true son of Abraham, needed baptism was to say something that had never been said, certainly never practiced before. Jesus might have passed it up as some new and useless fad.

He might have openly criticized John and his whole revival effort. He could have pointed out that many of the decisions were being made under great emotional stress, that the chances were better than two to one that many of those who were making professions and were being baptized would become nonresident members. Two years from the date they were baptized, few would be even making a pretense at living up to their commitment. Too, he could have pointed out that John's preaching was negative; it was a sounding of don'ts and shall nots. John seemed more concerned about what man should not do than he was with what God was able to do. He was thundering against man's sin instead of pleading God's grace. The note of repentance that John sounded so emphatically was not neglected in the preaching of Jesus, but certainly the major emphasis in the preaching of Jesus was different. And *it* is the emphasis that we remember. Longfellow contrasted the men in these verses:

> A voice by Jordan's shore!
>   A summons stern and clear;—
> Reform! be just! and sin no more!
>   God's judgment draweth near!

> A voice by Galilee,
>   A holier voice I hear;—
> Love God! thy neighbour love! for see,
>   God's mercy draweth near!

> O voice of Duty! still
>   Speak forth; I hear with awe;
> In thee I own the sovereign will,
>   Obey the sovereign law.

> Thou higher voice of love,
>   Yet speak Thy word in me;
> Through duty let me upward move
>   To thy pure liberty!

Consenting to   There was a third approach
Conform   that Jesus could have taken
                                     to John's preaching, to the
revival, and to the baptizing. This was what he did. He went
to John and said, "I wish to be baptized." What a strong and
tender sight it must have been. Luke puts it this way: "Now
when all the people were baptized, and when Jesus also had
been baptized." Does this mean that Jesus at first stood
unnoticed in the crowd, listened to the preaching, watched
reactions of the people, and rejoiced in the results? Then after
praying to the Father, just as John baptized the last candidate, did Jesus walk out to John, still standing in the Jordan,
and request baptism? Why?!

He did it as an act of renunciation—but not as a renunciation of sin. Christian faith finds it impossible to believe that
in requesting John's baptism, Jesus was repenting of sin. His
challenge, "Which one of you convicteth me of sin," has never
been seriously questioned. We are able to believe that he was
tempted in all points as we are tempted, but with the writer
of Hebrews we go on to affirm, "yet, without sin." We
respond warmly to the lines in John Oxenham's little
poem:

> He was a boy—like you—and you—,
>   As full of jokes, as full of fun,
> But always He was bravely true,
>   And did no wrong to anyone.
>
> And one thing I am sure about—
>   He never tumbled into sin,
> But kept himself, within, without,
>   As God had made Him, sweet and clean.[1]

Christians have not denied the difficulty of this position;
they have only recognized the greater difficulty in any other

position. It is the view based on Scripture. Also, followers of Jesus have never claimed that this position could be maintained apart from Christian faith.

As Jesus was not renouncing sin, neither was he renouncing a life of waste and uselessness. Even as a carpenter he had been "about his Father's business," and when the voice from heaven said of him "I am well pleased," it must have referred to all he had done. Both he and his work were in the center of God's will; the work was helpful to man, and it honored God.

He was renouncing the quiet life, the family joys, the simple if arduous responsibilities of making plows and yokes in the shop. In the place of these, he was assuming the dreadful responsibility of making and remaking men out on the horizons of God's great world. It was Erasmus who said that by a Carpenter mankind was made, and only by a Carpenter could mankind be remade. In the baptismal experience, Jesus was renouncing the strong guidance of Joseph, the loving care of Mary, the simple comforts of home, the kind if sometimes dull teaching of the synagogues, the warm if uncultured greetings of neighbors in and around Nazareth, the haunts where he had observed the flowers of the fields and watched the birds of the heavens. He was going out as one who had not where to lay his head, going out to become one who would be despised and rejected of men, one acquainted with grief, even to one day hanging on a cross.

Both Good and Bad

This scene at the Jordan represented not only an act of renunciation, it also represented an act of involvement. And just here is one of the areas where modern man is so unlike the Master. Modern men—you and I—do not like to become involved. For ex-

ample, in the predawn darkness in New York City, a young
woman by the name of Kitty Genovese was being stalked by a
killer. At last he stabbed her; then he left, returned, and
stabbed her again and again. It took thirty-five minutes for
him to kill her. Forty of her neighbors were roused by her
screams; they saw her being stabbed, but no one helped, no
one called the police. . . . On a bridge between San Pedro
and Terminal Island in Los Angeles harbor, California, two
highway patrolmen grappled with a man bent on suicide.
They needed help. They called to passing motorists, but no
one stopped. . . . In Riverside, California, a young woman
on her way home from church was dragged into a field where
she was choked and raped. Headlights from passing automo-
biles picked out the young woman and her attackers. No one
stopped. . . . In a building in the Bronx, New York, an
eighteen-year-old switchboard operator ran naked and hyster-
ical down a stairway into a vestibule. She was in plain sight of
a crowd gathered on the sidewalk. Olga Romero bled and
screamed as her rapist tried to drag her back upstairs. No one
helped; no one even called the police.

Witnesses to the two rapes and the murder told police later,
"I didn't want to get involved." It was probably the same
among those who saw the patrolmen struggling on the bridge.
This extreme desire for noninvolvement is a symptom of life
today. Dr. Edward Stainbrook, psychiatrist, says, "One no
longer values other individuals. They don't know them, so
they aren't concerned about them." Dr. Edward Walker,
police inspector, says, "Thousands of persons can live in one
building and not pay any attention to the next person. They
just don't want to get involved with him." Dr. Svend Riemer,
sociology professor, says, "Part of the personality of the big
city is not wanting to be involved. There is little cohesion
between people. They don't worry about the other guys." [2]

We do not want to get tied up, tied down; we do not want our liberty curtailed; we do not want to become involved in the corruption of city government and politics, with the race issue and the "poverty pockets." Middle-aged people are single and lonely because they are afraid of becoming involved; young, healthy, capable married couples are childless because they do not wish to become involved; multitudes live isolated lives in giant apartment buildings, not knowing the names of their neighbors even on the same floor because they do not wish to become involved. So we go on living our self-centered lives in our own little backwaters or eddies, refusing to step out into the muddy, rushing, whirling, confusing waters of the Jordan and become involved!

Not so the Master. He wished to identify himself with and to become involved in all of life. He said, "He who is not against me is for me." What if John's preaching and emphasis were different from his; what if it did sound a note that was more of the past than of the present and the future? John came neither eating nor drinking; Jesus came doing both. John lived his life in the desert wilds; Jesus lived his among the thronging multitudes. John was a voice crying in the wilderness; for a time, Jesus was the most popular dinner guest in all Palestine. But what of all this? John was a man who stood foursquare for God; he was a flaming witness; he had the eye and the ear of the people; he was emphasizing truths that had been neglected since the day of the prophet Amos; he had the courage of a lion and the passion of a red-hot furnace!

Years later Paul would write to Philippi: "What then? notwithstanding, every way . . . Christ is preached; and I therein do rejoice, yea, and I will rejoice." By his words and his actions Jesus wanted to show that *he* rejoiced; he was grateful; he wanted John to know. Jesus wanted John to know that he expected to be a part of the remedy and not a part of the problem. He would become involved with John and in this work that John was doing.

It is fearfully easy to criticize. The words are chosen with care. It is easy to criticize, and it is a fearful thing to do. Because you do not like the cut of the captain's hair or the sound of his uncultured voice or his uncouth manners, you may refuse to serve in the army of the King. In so doing, you may give aid and comfort to the enemy while the captain may be giving all and the best that he has. A man once criticized Dwight L. Moody's evangelistic methods. Moody admitted that he was not altogether pleased with them himself and asked the man what methods he would suggest. "Well," hedged the man, "I do not have any methods to suggest." "Then," said Mr. Moody, "I like my methods better."

Dr. Leslie Weatherhead, the distinguished former minister of City Temple, London, once wrote:

I well remember conducting a mission at the University of Leeds. After each session there was an opportunity for private conversations. A girl who was about to take her final degree examinations said something like this: "When I get back home, I know that the hardest thing in my religious life will be to stick with the services in our little village chapel. . . . So," she added, "I think I shall simply go up to the hills or into the woods. I shall more easily find God there . . ." Of course I told her that would never do as a rule. God ceases too soon to be real when we evade men, especially fellow-seekers, and seek Him selfishly for ourselves; and I reminded her of Him who was in the synagogue on the Sabbath day *as His custom was.* I reminded her that He must have had to listen to some pretty poor stuff from those old Rabbis; but that if others lifted their heads during the prayers and saw His face, they would come again; that in any case when He was there, it would be easier to pray; that she had something to give in a service as well as to get; and that her minister would break his heart if she deserted him instead of helping him to make the service what both wanted it to become. Since that date, the spiritual life of that little village church has been transformed and renewed, and it has overflowed to another village. The girl not only attended regularly but started a group which has become the spiritual powerhouse of the neighborhood.[3]

Jesus not only became identified with and involved in all that was good, he identified himself with and became involved in all that was bad. After two thousand years the scene still shocks us! The sinless Christ wades out into the muddy waters of Jordan to be baptized at the hands of sinful (for he was only man) John.

Sinlessness approaches the sinful; strength goes out to weakness; the divine goes out to the human; God goes out to man! Here is an example, a thumbnail sketch, of what his entire life and his death would be. He was a friend of publicans and sinners; he was numbered with the transgressors; he bore the sins of many. He came to save not the righteous but the sinners; he did not come to minister to the well but to the sick. Augustine said that God had one son on earth without sin but never one without suffering. "It was fitting," wrote the author of Hebrews, "that he [God], for whom and by whom all things exist, in bringing many sons to glory, should make the pioneer of their salvation perfect through suffering" (2:10, RSV).

In his baptism Jesus became involved with the world's evil and suffering. Men and women need to know this truth. Listen to Jeanne D'Orge writing in the *New York Times:*

I wish there were someone
Who would hear my confession.
Not a priest—I do not want to be told of my sins;
Not a mother—I do not want to give sorrow;
Not a friend—she would not know enough;

Not a lover—he would be too partial;
Not God—he is too far away;
But someone who would be a friend, lover, mother, priest, **God,**
    all in one,
And a stranger besides—who would not condemn or interfere;
Who, when everything is said from beginning to end,
Would show the reason of it all
And tell you to go ahead
And work it out your own way.[4]

As basic biblical theology, those lines may lack something; but as a cry of the human heart, it speaks to our condition. In its pervading tone, it points to One who involved himself with all that was bad.

Call to   Again, his baptism was an
Consecration   act of consecration. In some
deep and significant way, **he** was doing here at the beginning of his active ministry what he did at the close of his human sojourn among men. In John 17 we hear him saying, "For their sake I consecrate myself." At his baptism we do not listen to these words; but by his life and actions, he was saying much the same thing—acting out his purpose.

He was consecrating himself to the service of men. He had been serving men as he worked in the carpenter shop in Nazareth. Yet, "life is more than meat, and the body is more than raiment." When God wants a man to make a plow, the man does not honor God by insisting that he be allowed to make a sermon. But this does not alter the fact that a sermon which is used of God to bring men into a saving relationship with him is more important than a plow that helps man to make more or better ears of corn, for life *is* more than bread. It was a new and a higher service to which Jesus was now dedicating himself. He would be preaching the gospel to the poor, proclaiming release to the captives, the recovery of sight to the blind; he would be setting at liberty those who were oppressed; and he would be proclaiming the acceptable year of the Lord. The Spirit of the Lord was coming upon him for that purpose.

One of the church fathers said, "The kingdom of Heaven, O man, requires no other price than yourself; the value of it is yourself; give yourself for it, and you shall have it." Let us say it reverently; this was true for Christ no less than for his followers. He could gain the kingdom of God on no other grounds. This, surely, should be enough to banish any pink-tea dreams that the kingdom can be gained in our day.

Gilbert K. Chesterton, that thorny thistle in the side of his own church as well as the churches of all persuasions, saw that many people feel the kingdom of God can be gained through criticism and complaint alone, that once a group has pronounced judgment upon other groups for what they have done or have not done, they have thereby qualified themselves for the kingdom. So Chesterton wrote,

> The Christian Social Union here
> Was very much annoyed;
> It seems there is some duty
> Which we never should avoid,
> And so they sing a lot of hymns
> To help the Unemployed.[5]

In the act of baptism, Christ was consecrating himself to conflict. There must have been irritations and conflicts in the carpenter shop. Probably human nature then and there was not very different from what it is here and now. G. A. Studdert-Kennedy has raised this question:

I wonder what he charged for chairs at Nazareth
And did men try to beat him down
And boast about it in the town—
"I bought it cheap, for half-a-crown
From that mad Carpenter"? [6]

What Christ consecrated himself to face in conflict, however, was something quite different. On the stage of history
during that first century, the world saw a cosmic paradox.
God himself had come to earth in the person of his Son to
redeem men from their sins. In times past God had spoken
through the prophets, but now he was ready to speak through
his Son. It was like the famous pattern of a three-act play.
Two acts had been played out. In the first act the characters
were introduced and the circumstances were given. The
second act showed the characters hopelessly entangled in sin
and conflict. Then God was ready to lift the curtain on the
third act; God's love and purpose were about to be revealed.
Against the dark clouds of sin, he placed a rainbow in his sky;
and men would marvel: "Behold, what manner of love the
Father hath bestowed upon us, that we should be called the
sons of God!"

But before the victorious climax, evil will struggle more
viciously than ever; and before that conflict is over, history's
darkest deed will be done. In that crime it will appear that
God has forgotten man, but the very opposite will be true.
That deed will be a sign that God has come in the person of
his Son to reveal God's love for man, and all the forces of evil
will recognize this and gird themselves for battle. They will
cry out, "What have we to do with thee, thou Jesus of
Nazareth? art thou come to destroy us? I know thee who thou
art, the Holy One of God!" So evil and God's Son will stand
toe to toe. On the first day of that mortal combat evil will
seem to win, and God's Son will appear to be completely

crushed. But never judge God's battles at the close of only the first day. With God there is always a third day! Christ was consecrating himself to and for this conflict.

Endless   His baptismal experience
Enduement   was also a time of enduement
for Christ. Christian faith has always cherished the description that the Gospel writers give us of this event. Matthew, Mark, and Luke recorded it as an event to be remembered and cherished by all believers. Here it is in Luke's words: "Now when all the people were baptized, it came to pass, that Jesus also being baptized, and praying, the heaven was opened, and the Holy Ghost descended in a bodily shape like a dove upon him, and a voice came from heaven, which said, Thou art my beloved Son; in thee I am well pleased."

Here is new and additional enduement. In his farewell speech to the children of Israel, Moses had spoken for God the words, "As thy days, so shall thy strength be." Strength from God is like the manna in the wilderness in this: it has to be received fresh each morning, and each person may take as much as he can use. There is no limit to the supply; there is only a limit to the capacity and the need of the individual. God had given to his Son all the light and power needed in the carpenter shop. Now as he faced additional need, God was ready to supply more strength.

This great truth is seen in several phrases. First, God was giving new light to his Son. "The heaven was opened"—new truth, new understanding, new insight into the purpose of God was promised. Inscribed on the Eddystone lighthouse on the English coast are the words, "To give light is to give life." In order to be the *life* of the world, Christ had to be "the light of the world." That Light was the light from heaven. That is why it could not be put out. John came "as a burning and shining light," and men were willing to rejoice in the light that John gave them for a season. The light, the truth, the testimony that Christ brought was greater. He was the Light that the world could not put out.

It seemed a small light. One man, a working man, a carpenter by trade, one who had grown up among them, one whose brothers and sisters they knew, one who came from a town and community of no repute and a country that was held in bondage by military power, was in John's words "the true Light, which lighteth every man that cometh into the world." No man who followed him ever walked in darkness. Two men once went out one night; one took a torch and the other did not. When they returned, the latter reported that he found nothing but darkness; but the other said, "Everywhere I went I found the light."

In his biography of St. Francis of Assisi, Chesterton says, "While it was yet twilight a figure appeared silently and suddenly on a little hill above the city, dark against the fading darkness. For it was the end of a long and stern night, a night of vigil, not unvisited by stars. He stood with his hands lifted . . . and about him was a burst of birds singing; and behind him was the break of day." [7] So, to some lesser degree, it has been with every "St. Francis" who has followed the Light that lighteth every man. And, to a much greater degree and very different dimension, the light came to Jesus at his baptism.

He was also endued with fresh power. The Spirit of God descended like a dove upon him. Of course power had been given to make good yokes, but the baptism power was given to make good men, a much greater requirement. For this task nothing less was, or is, required than the presence and power of God. Writing about General Charles Gordon, a devout follower of Christ, one person said that the Sunday before the general left England for the Sudan, he "drove around to a number of churches to take communion as many times as possible, and thus start brimful of God." One may doubt that such was the purpose of the good general; witnesses must be God-filled, however, if good men are to be made.

> Did He call Lazarus back from death's abyss?
> Did He turn water into wine that wedding day?
> Yes, but His greatest miracle was this:
> To make a Christian from our common clay.[8]

We are told that there was also a "voice came from heaven." Here is new communication, too. This is a distinct ministry of Christ. He knew the Father; he communicated with the Father. John called him the "Word": "In the beginning was the Word, and the Word was with God, and the Word was God." Christ was the communications link between God and man.

To the Jew, a word was more than mere communication; it was something active, dynamic, creative; it did things; it had an existence of its own. The spoken word was something alive, charged with power. Sir George Adam Smith, the great Bible scholar, tells of meeting a group of Arabs on one occasion who greeted him with, "Peace be unto you," the regular salutation for one of their own. Later the Arabs discovered that Dr. Smith's party was made up of Christians. The Moslem Arabs then returned to Dr. Smith and begged for a restoration of the blessing; they did not want those active, creative, words to do their beneficent work in the lives of Christians.

Jesus said that no one knew the Father but the Son and no one knew the Son but the Father. The communication between the Father and the Son was of a nature the earth could not understand. It was the distinct work of Jesus to impart this understanding to men. To this undertaking he gave himself; to accomplish this task he died.

Another step was required. The word from heaven said, "This is my beloved Son, in whom I am well pleased." Here is approval, divine approval. It is approval for the past; what Jesus had done in Nazareth and the carpenter shop was good. The decision that Jesus had made to leave the carpenter shop and the pleasures of home was good. The decision of the Son to identify himself with all that was good and with all that was bad was good. God was well pleased.

In his book *Jesus Came Preaching* George Buttrick has called attention to the famous picture in the Boston library which shows the young Galahad approaching the throne seat that was said to rob a man of his life. Carved on the chair are the words, "He who sits herein shall lose himself." Galahad is shown moving forward; the knights of the Round Table watch his movements and stand in awe as they make the sign of the cross with their uplifted sword hilts. At the throne an angel has drawn back the red coverlet from the chair. You can almost hear the young knight saying, "If I lose myself, I save myself."

"This is my beloved Son," said the voice from heaven, "in whom I am well pleased." Christ had come for the purpose of losing himself; in losing himself he saved others.

3
"Not by Bread Alone"
Mark 1:1–13; Matthew 4:1–11; Luke 4:1–13

When the author of the book of Hebrews wanted to encourage his readers in their time of persecution, he did so by assuring them that Jesus, their High Priest, was not unmindful of their weakness, for he too had been tested as they were being tested. Phillips translates that verse: "For we have no superhuman High Priest to whom our weaknesses are unintelligible—he himself has shared fully in all our experience of temptation, except that he never sinned." [1]

So the tempted and tested of all ages have gone to Jesus and have found comfort ("with strength") in the assurance that by virtue of his own suffering under temptation, he is able to help all those who are being tempted now. It may seem strange, but those who have been broken on the wheel of life have found as much comfort in the humiliation of Christ as they have in his exaltation, as much in his voluntary weakness as in his God-endowed strength. Man, tempted and crushed, may not be able to understand Christ's glory; but he can understand Christ's sufferings. It was this that the loving wisdom of God saw; it was this which prompted the Father to send the Son. James Russell Lowell put it in memorable verse:

His magic was not far to seek—
He was so human! Whether strong or weak,
Far from his kind he neither sank nor soared,
But sat an equal guest at every board:
No beggar ever felt him condescend,
No prince presume, for still himself he bare
At manhood's simple level, and where'er
He met a stranger, there he left a friend.

In thinking of the temptation experience of Jesus, then, we come to the third recorded word or event in the life of Jesus. It was another giant hour for him. In the Temple he had become aware in some strange (and for us unclear) way of who he was. In the baptismal experience, he had known God's approval and had registered full commitment. In his temptation in the wilderness, he came to a new comprehension. It was not a comprehension of what his mission was to be so much as a comprehension of how that mission was to be accomplished.

Let us look at the setting and try to answer some questions that naturally come to mind when reading the account. First a word about time. All the writers of the incident affirm that it took place just after the baptismal experience. It is true to life that after a great experience there comes a reaction, the pendulum swings. Not only must a boat know the crest of the waves; it must also experience the troughs.

After Elijah's mountaintop experience in his victory over the priests of Baal came his flight into the desert and his juniper bush of discouragement. "Let him that thinketh he standeth take heed lest he fall." At the foot of the mountains of transfiguration stretch the valleys of humiliation. This truth is based on more than the natural reactions of our nervous system and the emotions that man has fallen heir to. Christian experience sees it as evil girding itself for battle on the heels of every satisfying divine-human encounter. The devil taunted God about Job saying that if he, the devil, could only get at Job, God would hear his faithful servant cursing him.

Desert **Encounter** The temptation took place in the desert not far from where Jesus was baptized. It was a stretch of desolate plateau, thirty-five by fifteen miles, known as The Devastation. It was made up of yellow sand, crumbling limestone, and scattered shale; the rocks were bare and jagged; the hills were dust heaps. In the day the sun made it a glittering furnace; at night the sounds were those of the howling jackals and the laughing hyenas. Every real temptation experience is partly subjective and partly objective. Surely the keen perception that could see in Peter the incarnation of evil and cry, "Get thee behind me, Satan!" would not require a physical being with hooves and horns and a forked tail with which to struggle.

One of the things that makes this incident so meaningful to the followers of Jesus in this: the Master would have to be the one who related it. Jesus was alone in the desert; we have the story only because he gave it to us. It is a significant chapter in his own spiritual biography. In it Jesus is telling us of his own soul struggle. Since this is true, it becomes one of the very meaningful and precious chapters of the New Testament.

We are told that the experience lasted forty days. For the Jews, forty was one of the *whole* numbers. Rain for forty days flooded the earth in Noah's time; Moses meditated on Sinai for forty days; Elijah was in the wilderness for forty days. Goliath challenged Israel for forty days; Jonah warned Nineveh of destruction within forty days. Jesus was in the wilderness of temptation for forty days.

We are told that Jesus was with the wild beasts. This fact enhances the story and lets us see a little more clearly the grim loneliness and desolation of the place. To some readers it may recall the prophecy of Hosea. "In that day," said the prophet, speaking for God, "I will make a covenant for them with the beasts of the field." If so, the import of the item is to point up, not the danger of the beasts to Jesus, but the fact that they were his companions in his lonely wilderness experience. Numerous incidents have been told of wild creatures showing no hostility to persons who were gentle and fearless toward them.

And we read that the "angels ministered unto him"—waited upon him, helped him. Of course they did. An angel is a messenger of God. When Elisha and his "ministerial student" were surrounded by the enemy at Dothan, Elisha prayed that God would open the young man's eyes. Seeing the horses and chariots of God all but covering the mountainside, he knew that those who were for them were greater than those who were opposed to them. Of Christ's prayer vigil in Gethsemane, Luke says, "There appeared an angel unto him from heaven, strengthening him." When Mark says that angels ministered to Jesus in his temptation experience, we are to understand that Jesus was not left to fight his temptations alone; he received help. So shall we.

We may wonder why Jesus was tempted in these three particular areas. The answer is that these were areas of his interest, concern, and strength. Had these not been areas of open possibility for Jesus, he would not have faced temptation in the way he did. The same is true for each of us; we are tempted along the line of our interest and strength. The record of the young women who were chosen as "Miss America" in the early days of the contest is not very good. There were divorces, frustrated careers, blasted dreams, failures in profession and in life generally. Because these young women had great beauty and charm, it was along that line that temptation pitched its battle. The same is true for physical strength. Samson came to his tragic end because he was unable to endure temptation in the area of his great physical strength. The skilled high school athlete who has a dozen universities competing for his attendance may be faced with temptations that the average youth knows nothing about. The brilliant speaker, the gifted writer, the actor or actress with great talent will find the temptation to prostitute these gifts having to be fought in some wilderness experience.

Take a look at the temptation itself. It was after Jesus had fasted forty days and was hungry that the devil presented his proposition. "If thou be the Son of God," he said, "command this stone that it be made bread." It is doubtful that physical hunger was the main battleground. It has been pretty well established that long before one has fasted this length of time the hunger pangs have ceased. So deeply engrossed in his mission was Jesus that he probably gave little attention to whatever sensations of hunger may have lingered. He could have found some type of food in the desert. We are told that for those who do not fear but trust her, the desert provides. There was no reason why Jesus could not have returned to the village if he had desired; he was not a hunted animal forced by law to remain away from his kind. He had gone into the wilderness voluntarily; he could have returned from the wilderness voluntarily.

Again, the chief area of conflict was not doubt. The devil had said, "If thou be the Son of God . . ." Much is often made of that "if." The point is emphasized that the devil was seeking to raise a doubt in the mind of Jesus as to his divinity, his relationship to God. It is the same idea that Christ faced on the cross when the thief shouted, "If thou be Christ, save thyself and us!" Yet, it was probably not a matter of doubting. Since Jesus was twelve, he had known that God was his Father in some very special way. Since his baptism, he had known God's unqualified approval. He was sure of the call that took him from the carpenter shop. He knew his mission in the world.

Means and   What he did not know was
Methods   just *how* this mission was to
                       be accomplished. What means
should he use in achieving God's purpose? Is this not one of your problems, too? You may have some doubts, but you are confident of the reality of God. You know that wrong is wrong, right is right. You know that your place is "on the side of the angels." You are quite sure that God will have the last word, and you desire to be there with him when he says it. Given a little time for careful and serious thinking, day or night, you would arrive at these positions.

The difficulty arises when you are called upon to make a decision about means and methods. How, where, when, and in what will you invest your life to bring about these desired ends? The crossroads of vocational choice is a crucial point on the highway of life; never forget it. However, this matter of ends and means, of methods and mission, will have to be faced again and again. Even after you have decided upon the main highway routing, there still remain many detours, side roads, cautions, curves, and stop signs along the way. Speed laws, ethics of the road, wayside ministries, and overnight accommodations will have to be decided. Often when a method and a means are decided upon, they will not stay decided but will have to be decided again and again.

The devil suggested that Jesus choose the means and method of bread for winning the world; "command this stone to become bread," he said. Meet the physical needs of men. That is what is important. Men are hungry. You can understand that for you are hungry. What is more, you live among people who are hungry; you see it; you feel it; you suffer because of it. The physical needs of men must come first. You cannot expect a man to be interested in prayer when he is hungry; you cannot expect a mother to be pious when her child is in pain for want of milk. Give men bread; show your concern; demonstrate your ability; and men will listen to you, follow you, trust you, serve you.

The world may question the wisdom of a man who refuses to satisfy his own hunger; it will have only contempt for the man who refuses to satisfy the hunger of others. A man may find grounds for voluntary fasting, but there is no justification for starving others. Is that not what a man does when he has the power to give men bread but refuses to do so?

This is something of what was involved in the temptation that Jesus faced—the temptation to turn stones into bread. It was an especially strong temptation because it came at the point of Jesus' awareness and concern. He did know the poverty-stricken condition of the people's lives. The typical American with his current normal living standard has no conception whatever of what the economic conditions were like in the Palestine of the first century.

G. A. Studdert-Kennedy wrote, "He was surrounded, I believe, by an innumerable phantom host of the world's hungry people. He saw them stretching out into the distance like an endless sea; mothers clasping puny children to their dry and shriveled breasts, fathers tearing open their ragged shirts to show the bones beneath their skin and holding out lean and skinny hands in supplication; while all around him, like the moan of the sea, there went up the cry of a world of want. 'Bread! Bread! For God's sake give us bread.' . . . If it ought to be done, he had no doubt it could be done. If it were God's will, then there must be God's way. Surely this was the most pressing and crying problem. Here was the greatest need—to feed the people. Was it any use to give them God unless he gave them bread? How could they worship unless they were fed? Was it not mockery to tell them of a Father's love unless he satisfied their human need?" [2]

Bread and the Messiah

There was, too, a strong conviction among the people that when the Messiah came, there would be bread for all; the hungry would be fed and the shelterless housed; each man would have his own vine and fig tree. Jesus was ever moved by the physical and material needs of men. He would later multiply the loaves and the fishes; he would say to his disciples, "They need not depart; you give them to eat." So concerned was he that he told a story of a rich man allowing a poor man to die at his gate for lack of food and medical care. In the parable Jesus left no doubt as to the way God would look upon such a case.

In the most dramatic of all his parables, Jesus pictured a scene at the judgment where men would be punished or rewarded according to how they dealt with the physical needs of men. In the parable he said that when men were hungry, they should be fed; when they were thirsty, they should be given drink; when they were naked, they should be clothed; when they were sick, they should be attended. So concerned was Jesus as to this point that he identified himself with the physical needs of men and said, "As you have done it unto one of the least of these my brethren, you have done it unto me."

An unknown writer prays in verse for God's compassion.

How many voices must be echoing in heaven, God,
How many sounds must beat upon your ears!
While I hear one man pouring out his fears,
The sorrowful chorus of the word is sung to you.

While I hear one bell tolling through the quiet night,
Millions of bells are clanging on high,
Billions of people shouting, "When?" "Where?" "Why?"
All day, each day, they scream their frenzied ravings to you.

Though the ceaseless noise of my small world seems deafening,
A universal din to you is raised;
With a banging, clanging noise you must be dazed
As the whirling wheels of time rush through the centuries.

But you should listen closely, God;
You should bend your head
And hear the hungry children
Whimpering, "Father, bread!"

Surely, surely, these ought to be fed. Surely, when God's
kingdom comes, they will be fed. If it is possible, why not
feed them now? This, I think, was the sharp point of the
temptation to turn stones into bread.

But Jesus refused to do it! "It is written," he said, "Man
shall not live by bread alone, but by every word that
proceedeth out of the mouth of God." He was saying that
there is a higher and a greater need than the physical. The
material comforts of life, are important only to the end that
higher needs be met. Life is more than an adequate diet, and
the body more than the latest styles.

Gerald Heard pictures Jesus answering the devil in penetrating words." Stones into loaves? Why not then the bitter
salt pools into milk—the sand into crystallized honey. And
they and I to settle down—the desert an easier acre than the

cornfield—eating and sleeping—working magic and then again feasting; until some king, learning of our secret, should carry us off as men keep bees and keep us as magicians at his court to feed his armies, we the first object of his enemy's attack; for, till we are destroyed, he is impregnable?" [3]

In Marc Connelly's *Green Pastures,* God "passes a miracle" when he makes "firmament." But finding he has made too much, God has to pass another miracle to dry up some of it. Then God says, "Dat's always de trouble wid miracles. When you pass one, you always gotta r'ar back an' pass another." [4]

The basic question that faced Jesus was this: Will man be better by possessing this miraculous power of making bread by miracle? Is it wise to revoke the divine word in Genesis that man is to live by the sweat of his brow, and instead let it be: man shall now live by miracle? Whatever may have been man's nature before his disobedience in Eden, there seems to be little doubt that work has been good for him since Eden.

> This is the Gospel of Labor—
> Ring it, ye bells of the kirk—
> The Lord of love came down from above
> To live with the men who work.
> This is the rose that he planted
> Here is the thorn–cursed soil—
> Heaven is blessed with perfect rest;
> But the blessing of earth is toil. [5]

Take another look at *Green Pastures.* In one scene God is talking to the angel Gabriel; he is disturbed because man seems to go from bad to worse. In spite of the flood, thunderbolts, and wrath, man continues his sinful way. Then God takes a new approach. He says to Gabriel:

"De good man is de man dat keeps busy. I mean I been goin' on de principle dat he was something like you angels—dat you ought to be able to give him somethin' an' den jes let him sit back an' enjoy it. Dat ain't so. Now dat I recollec' I put de first one down dere to take keer o' dat garden an' den let him go ahead an' do nothin' but git into mischief. Sure *dat's* it. He ain't *built* jes to fool 'round an' not do nothin'." [6]

Jesus declared that his Father worked and that he worked; it was essential that he work the works of his Father while it was day, for the night was coming when no one would be able to work. The old proverb says, "An idle brain is the devil's workshop," and Satan still has work for idle hands to do.

Kahlil Gibran, that gifted son of Lebanon, gave a spiritual insight into the purpose of work where he said:

Then a ploughman said, Speak to us of Work.
And he answered, saying:
You work that you may keep pace with the earth and the soul of the earth.
For to be idle is to become a stranger unto the seasons, and to step out of life's procession, that marches in majesty and proud submission toward the infinite.

When you work you are a flute through whose heart the whispering of the hours turns to music.
Which of you would be a reed, dumb and silent, when all else sings together in unison?

Always you have been told that work is a curse and labour a misfortune.
But I say to you that when you work you fulfill a part of earth's furthest dream, assigned to you when that dream was born,
And in keeping yourself with labour you are in truth loving life,
And to love life through labour is to be intimate with life's inmost secret. [7]

God is a worker; Jesus was a worker. Man is made in God's image. Man was meant to be a fellow-worker with God in the creation of bread. When the material needs of man are met without this working relationship, something is lacking.

Deficient in Vitamins

Unearned bread does not satisfy; it does not nourish man's better self. Somehow this unearned bread is deficient in emotional, moral, and spiritual vitamins; man suffers. Man's body may be fed while his self-respect is suffering. His body may be fed, but his independence and liberty may be destroyed. If a man has a fuller stomach, a more fashionable coat, a more modern roof, but thereby loses his self-respect, his right to stand on his own feet, and make his own contribution to his family, then bad is that man's bargain.

To be better off does not mean that a man is necessarily better. Those in the forefront of programs to alleviate poverty have often realized this. Speaking on behalf of President Johnson's "War Against Poverty," Assistant Secretary of Labor Daniel Patrick Moynihan has said, "Welfare has made poverty more endurable instead of providing a door of escape from it." [8] He points out that some families have been on relief for three or four generations. He says that the only way out of poverty for a man is employment. That is, man must have bread, but not bread without his own creative and creating effort, not handouts and doles, but a society and an economy that gives him a chance to work and to produce.

Now, in spite of Eden, the example of Christ, the poets, the wise old folk sayings, and our own experience, modern-day thinking will have none of it. Work is a curse; leisure is a blessing. The fewer hours man works, the better is his condition. Pity the tired workman; envy the idle hands;

equate work with tragedy and worklessness with blessing. Find a way, any possible way, to magically turn stones into bread and keep the sweat from man's brow. Watch the clock; take it easy; slow the assembly line.

Or, on the other side, emphasize automation; speed up the assembly line; treat the worker as a cog in the necessary mechanical production line; give first attention to profits, dividends, and capital gains. Much of modern business is a rather heartless affair whether it is viewed from the standpoint of the worker or the manager. Much of it has the flavor of the conversation in the wilderness between the devil and the Son of God; the battle still goes on today. It goes on not only in big business, but also among the professions: medicine, scientific research, teaching, and others.

Still, sometime ago when an English newspaper made a survey asking the question, "Who are the happiest people in the world?" the following four answers won the day: a craftsman whistling over a job well done, a child building sand castles, a mother bathing her baby, a doctor finishing a difficult but successful operation.

There is no guarantee that men will be good and wise just because they are rich and comfortable. Bread and righteousness are not the same thing, no matter what the arguments from Satan, the labor leader, the chairman of the board, or the leader of the crusade or boycott say. It may be hard for a man to pray on an empty stomach, but there is no proof that he will be any more likely to pray on a full stomach.

Listen to the ancient words of Deuteronomy:

When the Lord thy God shall have brought thee into the land . . . to give thee great and goodly cities, which thou buildedst not, and houses full of all good things, which thou

filledst not, and wells digged, which thou diggedst not, vineyards
and olive trees, which thou plantedst not; when thou shalt have
eaten and be full; *Then beware lest thou forget the Lord.*

Every experienced pastor knows the sad story. A man works
hard; he is faithful to home, friends, church, and God.
Financial success comes his way. He finds new associates; he
joins the country club set and the cocktail circuit. The home
is broken; friends are forgotten; the church is neglected; and
God is betrayed. Of course these things, many of them,
happen among the hard laborers, too; no one denies that. But
to be better off is not the same as being better. Man cannot
live by bread alone. The devil insinuated that he could;
Christ affirmed that he could not. The lines are drawn. Who
gets your vote—your vote not just of word but of conduct?

If man can have the material possessions of life at will—by
miracle and without labor—he will take them as the goal of
life and not just the means for achieving a really worthy goal
in life. A bold statement? Indeed, it is! Yet, take a careful
look at history; study the rise and fall of civilizations; have a
good long dialogue with Mr. Toynbee. Listen to the psalmist:
"But [they] lusted exceedingly in the wilderness, and tempted
God in the desert. . . . [so] he gave them their request; but
sent leanness into their soul" (106:14–15).

"Man does not live by bread alone." He lives by every
word, call, and challenge of God upon his mind and heart. If
he does not do this, he is little better than the beasts of the
field—the dog burying his bone, hoarding it until a later
hour. He is not as one joining the pilgrim band that marches
toward the city that "hath foundations whose builder and
maker is God." Henry S. Canby wrote:

We are scientific, utilitarian, practical. . . . But no one of us
is all scientific, utilitarian, practical. The waters still run deep,

even though the angel of the Old Testament seldom troubles them. A craving for beauty, a sense of awe, a moral urge, the love of an ideal, the need of worship, the belief in spiritual values, are of course as existent in a machine age as in any other . . . They must find expression somehow.[9]

In *Between Tears and Laughter,* Lin Yutang reminded us that things neither make for greatness, nor do they satisfy a craving to create it. The Barretts of Wimpole Street did not have the luxury of enameled bathtubs; Charles Dickens never turned the knob of a radio; Goethe never clicked the shutter of a camera; Dryden's room was neither steam-heated nor cooled by refrigeration; Bill Shakespeare never read a newspaper, nor did he ever attend the movies.

Man is a spiritual being as well as a material animal. He cannot live long without bread, but neither can he live by bread only. This life is temporary; man was meant to prepare for another life. "All this life," said Heard, "man must be learning to diet himself for another way of living."

Within the womb before his birth man developed eyes, but there were no colors for him to see; he developed ears but had no harmonies to enjoy; developed feet though there were no paths of service for him to walk, and hands though there were no deeds of usefulness for him to perform. Just so, man was meant to grow "spiritual organs" while he is here on this earth. Through the experience of birth man emerged into a world where every normal growth and development within the womb might be employed and enjoyed. So, through Christian faith, man is convinced that there is a life and an experience beyond this life; and the hopes, the dreams, and the sensitivities that could find no adequate expression in this life will know complete fulfilment then.

It is as necessary for man to develop his capacities here for that world as it was for the child to develop sensory organs in the womb for fulfilling his role here after physical birth. But this growth, this nurture, cannot be satisfied with bread only; it is God's word, God's call, God's challenge, God's grace which supplies the necessary ingredients for this part of man's diet.

"Command that these stones be made bread," said the tempter. "It is written," said Jesus, "Man shall not live by bread alone, but by every word that proceedeth out of the mouth of God." The position of the two candidates is clear. It is time to cast your ballot. How do you vote?

4
"Yes, and
the Scriptures Also Say"
MATTHEW 4:1–11

Since Jesus had bested the tempter in the matter of stones and bread, we might think that the Son of God would not have been tested again. But Satan does not accept defeat just in losing one battle. He offered Jesus a second temptation. When you and I are faced by the same old foe—the one we have resisted in the past time and again—we may take comfort in the fact that Jesus experienced that, too.

On this occasion Jesus was tempted to use sensational methods to secure attention. In his mind, Jesus saw the court of the Temple thronged; a feast day was at hand. In imagination he stood on the pinnacle of the Temple and looked down. All eyes were lifted to him. The devil said, "Cast thyself down: for it is written, He shall give his angels charge concerning thee: and in their hands they shall bear thee up, lest at any time thou dash thy foot against a stone."

The question was: How would Jesus attract the attention of the people so that they would hear his message from God? What is the good of having a message if you do not deliver it? Why preach if no one listens? Attention is necessary. Only the person who can capture the attention of an audience has a chance to make his message clear and convincing. At the beginning of his ministry Jesus was asking: How can you make people listen?

The tempter replied: "Throw yourself down. If you will cast yourself from this pinnacle and go floating down to the crowd, every eye will be upon you, and every ear will be ready to hear what you say. The people will then know—and find it impossible to doubt—that you are different from all other men. They will know that you are God's chosen one, that you have been sent to deliver them. They will know that you are destiny's darling. Because the leap will bring no harm to you, they will see that you are God's favorite. It is true. You *are* different from all other men. You are God's chosen one; you are sent to deliver the people. He will protect you. You have the promise of the care of the angels."

According to the reasoning of the tempter, his plan would accomplish several things. It would demonstrate once and for all that Jesus trusted God completely. It would demonstrate beyond any doubt that Jesus was willing to be used of God. Again, it would be a final proof of God's love for and protection of his Son. Because God loved, of course God would protect. He could not afford to do anything else. After all, the Son would be trusting the Father completely.

The motives of the Son would be the highest; he would not be doing this for himself but only to fulfil the intention of God. This plan would prove then that Jesus was in the plan and purpose of God, that God approved the words and deeds of his Son, and the people would know once and for all that the Father and the Son were in the mission together. Finally, it would end forever any lingering doubts that Jesus might have about his sonship. Nothing can undo a man more thoroughly and completely than doubts. Let us get this faith nailed down and thoroughly bradded!

Satan came to his climax: "Do it now! Jump! Jump!"

But Jesus refused to jump! It was not easy for him to refuse. How could he see through the proposition so clearly! He wanted the ear of the people; he deserved their attention; he alone had a message for the people that was wholly worthy and completely adequate. The people were tired and weary; they were depressed and frustrated. It was difficult to get their attention, and to get their interest was almost too much to hope for. They loved the spectacular and sensational. He would not have been doing it for himself; the tempter said nothing about his motive. Besides, there was a belief among the people that when the Messiah came, he would come floating down from the clouds.

Jesus surely knew that so far as being given any sort of place of leadership and responsibility by the religious leaders of the day, his case was hopeless. He did not bear the brand of their schools, nor did he have the accent of their doctrines nor the inflection of their theology. He knew he would have to make his own way, head up his own campaign. The tempter's proposition seemed to be just what he needed at the very beginning of his ministry. All he had to do was to jump.

The Hidden Evil   What was the hidden evil? It was an effort to put God on the spot. See how it went. Jesus was God's Son; God was his Father. He was doing God's will for God's glory. For the Son to fail would be the same as failure for the Father. Had Jesus yielded to this temptation, one of three things would have been clear in the minds of the people. First, God could save his Son and would; second, God would save his Son if he could, but he could not; third, God could save his Son if he would, but he would not.

The sharp mind and clear moral judgment of Jesus saw the temptation for what it was. It was not an effort to have Jesus *trust* God; it was an effort to have Jesus *test* God. It would not be an expression of faith, but the expression of a threat.

Never make the effort to see how far you can go with God. The safe driver is not the one who sees how close he can drive to the edge of the cliff without going over; the safe driver is one who keeps his car safely away from the edge of the cliff. The trusting Christian is not the one who thrusts his hand in the fire to test the power of God; he is the one who respects fire as a creation of God and treats that creation with caution. The true follower of Christ is not one who voluntarily goes into the den with wild beasts for sensational purposes, nor picks up poisonous snakes to show the protection of God, nor recklessly drinks arsenic because he thinks the love of God makes him immune to its deadly effects.

God expects his followers to be loyal to him. If in being loyal the believer is thrown into prison, cast into flames, thrown to wild beasts, forced to drink poison, or torn asunder, God promises deliverance. Deliverance always comes, if not *from* these dangers, then in and through these dangers. If God does not bring his child out of the flames, God will go into the flames with his child. This he has done a thousand times for his saints and martyrs. It is one thing to trust God and, because of that trust, be thrown from "the pinnacle of the temple"; it is something else again to throw yourself from the temple to show that you are God's pet. The first is God-honoring; the second is self-glorification.

The righteous nation is not one that heedlessly goes its own selfish way, ignoring the commandments of its God in the realm of ethics and morals, greedily squandering its good name and its good will among the peoples of the world for a mess of financial pottage, ignoring the rights and dignities of large sections of its people for an inherited tradition and prejudice, allowing crime to breed and corruption to flourish in a thousand high places, yet in any national or international emergency confidently calling upon its God to bear it up lest it dash its national foot against the stone of circumstances and moral law. Don't be fooled; God cannot be cheated: for whatever a nation sows, that shall it also reap.

Also, a church should trust God; test God, it should not. Obey God, it should; try God, it should not. It is fearfully easy for a church to become complacent and self-centered. It may well lose its first love and passion. And make no mistake, the "first love" for a church, even as for an individual, is its relationship with God in Christ. It is as easy for a church to lose this love through busy activity as through indifferent inertia. There was no lack of works, orthodoxy, or patience on the part of the church at Ephesus, but it was still warned about leaving its first love. A church, as well as the individual Christian, must love the Lord its God with all its heart, soul, strength, and mind; it must love its neighbor as itself. And the loves must come in that order. If the church neglects either, it has forfeited its right to existence as a Christian church.

It is difficult for a church to change its course, to mend its ways. Old habits are strong; old ways of doing things are comfortable—comfortable like an old bedroom shoe. Not only is it difficult to change; it may be too late to change—not too late from God's point but from the church's point. In Lederer and Burdick's novel, *The Ugly American,* Major Monet says, "That's enough, gentlemen. Even if you're right we don't have time to change our tactics. We're losing too fast." [1] That may well be true of churches.

In *The Shoes of the Fisherman,* the Pope is speaking to Semmering about Jean Télémond. The Pope wonders if Télémond is justified in taking the risks that he takes. To this, Semmering answers: "If a man is centered upon himself, the smallest risk is too great for him, because both success and failure can destroy him. If he is centered upon God, then no risk is too great, because success is already guaranteed—the successful union of Creator and creature." [2] That is not only a true and wise observation; it is a thrilling word, a word of faith. It reminds us of the words of the Hebrew youths who, when threatened by the king with being thrown into the burning furnace, answered: "We would not make any defense in this matter; for the God whom we serve is able to save us from the fire of the furnace and He will deliver us out of your hand, O king. But, whether He does or not, be it known to you, O king, we will not serve your gods, or worship the image which you have set up." [3] There you have the sound of the trumpet from the "hid battlements of Eternity"!

To the young Hebrews, it was a small thing whether God saved them from the furnace or not. They knew that he could save them; that was all they asked. They were willing to leave the wisdom of such a deliverance to him. Whatever might happen to them in the furnace would not alter the fact that God was God, that nothing could change God's character. Surely Jesus knew this. The devil might contend that God was required to give physical protection to those who trusted him; Jesus did not so contend. God could allow a body to be broken, especially if that body was foolishly ventured, without God's integrity being brought into question.

Jesus never yielded to the popular "cult of success" which says that success is good and failure is bad. Whatever is required to succeed is justifiable, for success is the highest good. However, the man who fails is a failure, regardless of the moral scruples which may have influenced him. T. S. Eliot speaks effectively to this in *The Elder Statesman*. Consider the penetrating words: "The worst kind of failure, in my opinion, is the man who has to keep on pretending to himself that he's a success—the man who in the morning has to make up his face before he looks in the mirror." [4] The "failure" of an individual, even of the Son of God, would not mean God's defeat. God could not be "put on the spot" with any such cheap showmanship! "Thou shalt not tempt the Lord thy God." If you do tempt him, you, not God, are responsible for the outcome.

Proviso in the Contract The temptation to leap from the pinnacle of the Temple was not only an effort to put God on the spot; it was an effort to put a proviso in the contract. The tempter was trying to get Jesus to put a conditional stipulation in the obedience agreement, the commitment document. See how it went. I am your Son; I am come to do your will and work. I am willing to do all that, *provided;* I will love you, provided; I will be obedient, provided; I will serve you, provided; I will witness for you, provided—provided you protect me from all danger. You must not let me get a broken leg in foolish leaps; you must not let me have an accident on the highways whether due to my carelessness, my poor judgement, the other driver's intoxicated state, the unsafe condition of the road, or the mechanical failure of one or both cars. You must not let my body become a lodging place for a cancer germ, a TB microbe, a defective heart, or a cushion for fallout.

Now, this agreement must extend to the members of my family and immediate relatives and a few of my close friends. Oh, yes, and I would like also some type of coverage for my business ventures. Of course, I have good precedent for this point. Remember the proviso Jacob proposed for his contract with God at Bethel? "Jacob vowed a vow, saying, If God will be with me, . . . and will give me bread to eat, . . . then shall the Lord be my God: . . . and of all that thou shalt give me I will surely give the tenth unto thee."

One of the great temptations of the Christian life is to try to force God to play favorites. When some people become followers of Christ, they seem to think that the laws affecting ordinary human beings should not apply to them. Gravity, bacteria, catastrophe should treat the non-Christian one way and the believer another way. If the non-Christian jumps from the pinnacles of the temple of law and order, he must pay the consequences. Not so for the Christian. But these foolish ones forget that God is no respecter of persons.

How easy it is to insist on provisos! How hard it is to leave the small print in the contract entirely up to God. We are so conditioned by the thinking of the secular world that it is difficult for us to shift gears when we come to God. We still want to ask what we shall get out of every agreement.

But this spirit has no place in man's relationship with God. No matter how many marriages are based on material gain, the mind—certainly the heart—knows that this is an improper and an unsafe basis for marriage. When a man bases his commitment to God on the protection that he gets, the increased income that may be expected, the higher rung on the social ladder that he may occupy, the smaller hospital bill that he may have to pay, the stronger and healthier body that he may enjoy, the better adjusted personality that he will have, he is yielding to a temptation that Christ resisted in the desert. No! Trust God and leave the provisos with him.

Merely Winning Attention

Had Jesus yielded, what would have been the results? Obviously, this is no place for the mind of mortal man to be proud. Yet it seems obvious that these results would have followed. He would have won the attention of the crowds. People then, not unlike ourselves, always responded to superman. The strongest man, the most beautiful woman, the fastest driver, the richest man, the best-dressed woman, the highest-paid movie star, the wonder worker—these always get attention. Jesus faced the problem throughout his entire ministry. They followed him because of the miracles they saw him perform, because of the loaves and fishes that he multiplied. They would have given him their attention had he leaped from the pinnacle of the Temple.

That is, they would have given him their attention for a time. Then it would have been necessary for him to perform some other stunt, something more remarkable. Miracles, like dope, call for a continuing increase in dosage. But it is doubtful that he would ever have won the hearts of the people even briefly with miracles alone. Paradoxical as it may seem, the crowds love a miracle worker, but they never feel very close to him. The miracles emphasize the gap between the ordinary person and the performer of the miracle. A subconscious jealousy prevents real devotion. C. P. Snow describes one of his characters in *The Masters* as one in whom intimacy could flow only one way. "He was so made that he could not bear the equality of the heart." So, from the standpoint of the mere miracle worker, the heart is evasive and cautious.

Not only for Jesus was this a severe temptation; it still threatens every earnest messenger of God's truth. Men are lonely, isolated, empty, drifting, rootless, lost, imprisoned. Jean Paul Sartre's play *No Exit* describes their condition. Three characters sit in a room; there is no escape from it. They find no satisfaction in one another; yet they are unable to escape from one another. The only thing that they can do is torment one another; for them it is "hell." Although the play

stopped there, we know the gospel of God has come, and it is
the only way of escape. The present-day young messenger has
the message, he knows the state of the people, and he knows
that the message can deliver them. But the people will not
listen. What will he do? He will be tempted, as Jesus was, to
use sensational means—a bag of tricks to get the ear of the
people—in order to give them the message that will release
them from their corporate and private "hells."

No Room for Again, if Jesus had yielded
Coercion to this temptation, he would
have been in the business of
coercing man's will. That Jesus refused to do. No one ever
understood man's tragic state as well as Christ; no one ever
wanted to deliver man from his tragic state as much as the
Master. Yet he refused, absolutely refused, to use coercion.
The sensational methods involved in the temptation of leap-
ing from the pinnacle of the Temple would pressure man's
will. It would have been like wringing a confession from man
against his calm, reasoned, and love-directed judgment.

The hard steel in the resolution of Jesus at this point is
frightening. Let it be said reverently, but it needs to be said:
Jesus preferred to let men remain in their sin rather than
coerce them into belief! He so honored man's freedom in the
area of the will that he felt it better to let men go to hell than
to force them in to heaven! Man's will is his own; God gave it
to him. Within the realm of the will, man is sovereign; God
ordained it so. When Pharaoh appointed Joseph prime minister, or secretary of food and conservation, he said: "Only in
the throne will I be greater than thou." The will is man's
throne. This should be relinquished to no one. God meant
for man to keep it inviolate.

"Behold, I stand at the door, and knock: if any man hear

my voice, and open the door, I will come in." That is how important Christ considers man's will. Ah, my soul! The strength of the Saviour is revealed not only in what he was willing to do to redeem man, but also in what he refused to do to redeem him. Man is made in the image of God. Man is so valuable to him that God sent his Son to save him. Man was given "dominion"; man is so great that God would not coerce him. Persuade man, yes, with the persuasion of Calvary, but let man be free to choose.

A few days after General Douglas MacArthur's death, Billy Graham, the evangelist, reported a private conversation he had had with the general. MacArthur said that Emperor Hirohito of Japan had talked with him shortly after Japan's surrender and declared his willingness to make Christianity the official religion of Japan. MacArthur had hesitated; the emperor asked him to think further about it. Later MacArthur had returned to the emperor with these words: "Never. No nation must ever be made to conform to any religion. It must be done voluntarily." Whatever may be the estimate of General MacArthur's later activities, whether you agree with his decisions and his conduct or not, there can be little doubt about his Christian thinking and decision in this instance. Man is, and by God-given right must be, free to choose life or death.

Freedom is both privilege and responsibility. It can be a weight as well as wings. Mass movements often flourish because individuals wish to escape individual responsibility. They desire freedom from freedom. The Nazis bitterly fought the idea that they were individually responsible for obeying orders. Nor is this state of affairs absent from the religious scene. Any system of religion that promises to be responsible for the salvation of the individual in return for that individual's freedom of thought and will has a great

advantage with multitudes. Multitudes are glad to exchange
freedom of choice in return for a "package deal" in the
salvation market. This idea is a travesty of true religion!
Christ would have none of it.

The will of man is never safe until it is yielded to God, but
it has to be *voluntarily yielded*.

> The will is free:
> Strong is the Soul, and wise, and beautiful:
> The seeds of godlike power are in us still:
> Gods are we, Bards, Saints, Heroes, if we will.

"If we will," those are the key words. We may almost accept
Matthew Arnold's uncharacteristic enthusiasm if we keep
those words clearly in mind. We need to pray the prayer of
Augustine: "O Lord, grant that I may do thy will as if it were
my will; so that thou mayest do my will as if it were thy
will."

Again, had Jesus yielded to Satan's temptation to use the
way of sensation and trickery, he would have been surrender-
ing his confidence in the magnetic power of the cross and the
way of the cross. Bishop Walpole, father of Hugh Walpole,
the novelist, once said to a friend who was weighing and
debating a call, "If you are uncertain of which two paths to
take, choose the one on which the shadow of the cross falls."
But this was just what the tempter was suggesting that Jesus
not do.

Jesus was weighing methods for reaching people with God's
message. Satan had first suggested that he use the method of
bread—material satisfactions. This, Jesus rejected. The devil
then suggested that Christ use the method of sensation and
wonder: startle the people with a dramatic descent from the
pinnacle of the Temple. The temptation here was not to
abandon the cross as an end; the devil was too wise to suggest

that. He was suggesting that Jesus use a sensational means for attaining his purpose in the cross. The tempter proposed: "While the way of service, sacrifice, and death may be your ultimate end, it need not be your immediate means. Once you get the attention of the people, the way of the cross may work; the Suffering Servant of Isaiah may be adequate then, but it will not secure the attention of the people now. You must have something more dramatic, sensational, magical."

For us the question is this: Must the spirit of the cross pervade all our means and promotional efforts as well as be the heart of our message?

Shortly before his crucifixion, Jesus said: "I, when I am lifted up . . . , will draw all men unto myself" (John 12:32, RSV). The way of the cross is the greatest drawing force for good the world has ever known. George Tyrrell once wrote to Baron von Hügel these haunting words: "What a relief if one could conscientiously wash one's hands of the whole concern! But then there is that Strange Man upon His Cross who drives one back again and again." It is a wonderful thing for a minister to feel the strong magnetic pull of that "Strange Man upon His Cross" in everything he does. There is no suggestion here that organization, administration, methods, and techniques be ignored. They should neither be ignored nor used haphazardly. The service of the king requires both haste and efficiency. We cannot be careless and inefficient in our work for God. Everything that will help us render better service should be, must be, used "in the spirit of the cross."

Means and methods must merge into one. "I will be unanimous," announced Henry David Thoreau when he was a boy. It is a good announcement, but most men cannot make it. They are divided in mind because it is so very easy to want the right things, want them desperately, so desperately that we are willing to use bad means to get them.

Difficulty of   But, you see, we can never
Drawing Lines   be very sure which are ends
and which are means in our
service for Christ. You minister to a sick body hoping that
you will get a chance to tell him about the love of the
Saviour; later you learn that you were actually ministering to
Jesus in the first place. You fight your way through a storm in
order to help someone and later find that it was the fighting
through the storm that was most helpful. A "Borden of Yale"
surrenders and sacrifices, studies and disciplines himself, in
order that he may glorify Christ and serve mankind. Just as he
is ready to go about that business, he dies. Then you learn
that it was the very means that he was using to reach the
desired end that were the greatest end. Just where will you
draw the line between ends and means for a "Bill Wallace of
China"?

What Van Wyck Brooks said of writing is true of Christian
living. "No good writer has ever liked drudgery," wrote
Brooks, "nor has any good writer ever permitted anyone else
to do his drudgery for him." So much of life, even the
Christian's life, is drudgery. Yet, the routine tasks are necessary. They cannot be avoided. They must be invested with
the Spirit of Christ. In *If I Go Down to Hell*, Malcolm Boyd
says: "It is no good trying to fool yourself about love. You
can't fall into it like a soft job, without dirtying up your
hands. It takes muscle and guts. And if you can't bear the
thought of messing up your nice, clean soul, you'd better give
up the whole idea of life." [5] Right! The cross is "messy
business."

When means and ends are not kept close and made to heel
to the spirit of the cross, a man's work becomes divided; and
what is even more serious, he becomes divided himself. His
work suffers. One man neglects means because it is only the

end result that he is concerned about. Another man becomes so involved in means that he never gets around to ends. In either case the cause of Christ suffers. A mother, for example, who needs help refuses to study, listen to her doctor, read books and magazines, or attend lectures; thus, she may not be really qualified to attend to her baby. On the other hand, a mother who gives all her time to these "preparations" and none to her husband, home, and child, may be an even less effective mother.

There are different ways of "tempting the Lord thy God." One is to give no thought to ends but only to means of reaching the end. But we tempt the Lord no less if we give no thought to methods and techniques. We expect the Lord to miraculously bear us and our work up lest we dash our feet against stones of failure, even though we have used neither brain nor brawn.

Yes, and the Scriptures also say: "Thou shalt not tempt the Lord thy God." Thou shalt trust him.

5
"Away with You, Satan!"

MATTHEW 4:1–11

In George Bernard Shaw's *Androcles and the Lion,* a perennial problem is brought into focus. The giant gladiator, Ferrovius, is a man of great strength and violence. When he becomes a Christian, he must choose between two different ways of life, the way of brutal conflict and physical dominance or the way of spiritual vitality and sacrifice. He is torn between the love of Christ and the service of Caesar. It is a difficult decision, but he makes it; and in making it, he says: "The Christian God is not yet. Meanwhile I must serve the gods that are. I take service with Caesar." Compromise!

Basically, this was the third temptation that Jesus faced in the wilderness. With his mind's eye Jesus saw the peoples of the world before him. They were restless and lost. He had the message that would bring them home to God and bring God and home to their hearts. How could the task be accomplished? Not through satisfying their physical desires; this way he had rejected in refusing to turn stones into bread. Not the way of cheap sensationalism; this he had rejected in refusing to cast himself from the pinnacle of the Temple. Would it be by compromise? by lowering his standards? by using the powers of evil to promote the powers of good? by choosing the service and worship of Caesar until the hour of the Christian God struck? This was the test.

**Motives and
Desires**

The temptation was strong —the strongest that he had faced, and for three reasons. First, the temptation was in the realm of motives and desires. When the tempter talked about the nations of the world being given over to Jesus, the tempter was speeding up the heart beat of the Master. This was the consuming passion of his heart. The note is sounded in the missionary hymn:

> The whole wide world for Jesus!
>   Its hearts, and homes, and thrones;
> Ring out again the watchword
>   In loud and joyous tones:
> The whole wide world for Jesus!
>   With pray'r the song we'll wing,
> And speed the pray'r with labor,
>   Till earth shall crown Him King.

It was not only his passionate desire; it was his purpose and goal. He expressed it in many ways, such as, "I came not to do my own will but the will of him who sent me," and "The Son of man did not come to be ministered unto, but to minister." He said that God loved the world so much that he had sent his Son that whoever would believe might have everlasting life; that instead of condemning the world, the Son had come to give life to the world. He said that he come that the people might have abundant life. He described himself as the Good Shepherd, the Water of life, the Light of the world, the Way, the Truth, and the Life. However it might be stated, the purpose and end were the same: Jesus came to bring the people back to God.

A medieval Latin Christmas carol calls upon all good Christian men to rejoice because Jesus Christ was born for this: to open heaven's door and to insure that man is blessed forevermore, for Christ was born to save; Christ was born for this. What the devil promised was what Christ came to accomplish.

Again, the tempter's promise of world dominion offered what the people really desired. They wanted a master, someone who would take the reins of power, assume authority over them and the nation. In return for this the people were willing to rebel against the Roman powers; they had done it again and again; they were willing to believe and follow anyone who promised, through almost any pipe dream, to lead them into God's kingdom. True, they may have been mistaken as to what that kingdom was meant to be, but to the best of their understanding they wanted that kingdom and were looking for someone to lead them into it.

Also, the devil offered what the Word of God endorsed. Christian faith has always laid hold of the promise that the heathen would be given to Christ for an inheritance, and the ends of the earth would be his possession. That every knee would bow and every tongue would confess him has been a part of our traditional faith. The churches have claimed to believe the dreadful word that there is no other name under heaven by which men may be saved except the name of Jesus. Individuals and groups may argue, reason, and rationalize about this position that the Bible takes, but the Bible is so clear and firm that he who runs may read. On one occasion a group of Christians was arguing hotly about missions. One man contended that it was not the will and purpose of God that every nation and people become Christian. When the speaker sat down, one old man stood up and said, "Rax me that Bible!"

Invitation of A second reason the tempta-
Circumstances tion was so strong rests upon
the circumstances. Evil had
made a mess of the nations. It always does. Satan is not only
evil, he is the father of lies. He bungles everything he puts his
hand, claw, fork, or dazzling light to. Christ could have done a
better job than Rome. Writing on this point, Leslie Weatherhead has said that under Christ "there would be justice
instead of oppression, there would be food instead of hunger,
there would be love and happiness among those smiling fields
instead of that dull sullen hate of a ruthless invader. What a
glorious cause he might have championed!" [1] The world was
ready for new leadership.

This is a point that the world will not accept: that sin is not
only sinful, it is foolish. Not only does evil not work for the
individual; it does not work for the institution, the nation, or
the world. It will not bring happiness, it will not bring
stability; it will not bring harmony; it will not even bring
enduring wealth or enduring political ascendancy.

In the long ago, when Judah's politicians were planning an
alliance with Egypt, Isaiah taunted them because they looked
to Egypt's cavalry and military might but not to the Holy
One of Israel. "Yet he also is wise," said Isaiah, "and will
bring evil, and will not call back his words."

F. Scott Fitzgerald, recognized spokesman for the jazz era,
said there were those in the 1920's who thought that life
was a game in which everyone was off side, the referee had
been chased from the field, and there were no rules. That is
not a bad picture of Satan's leadership. The only thing that
holds even thieves together is the little honesty and integrity
that exists among them.

Can any fair-minded individual look at today's world and
believe that evil has enough wisdom to direct this world to

any creative and worthy ends? Look at crime, gambling, dope, race, communism, graft, greed, sex, broken homes, confused education, rudderless politics. On the cross Jesus prayed for his crucifiers not only because they were bad, but also because they were stupid. He said: "Father, forgive them; for they know not what they do." Evil gives to man what he thinks is the Rachel of his heart's desire; man wakes up and finds he has Leah instead! No matter how quickly evil promised to reward the appetite of Isaac, it turned out to be sly and cunning Jacob beneath the coarse hands and the disguised voice that sounded so much like Esau. Wise is the man who can detect the difference between the devil's promise and his ultimate product.

In those tragic days following World War I, when the government in Washington was all but paralyzed because of the illness of President Wilson, Senator Albert B. Fall of New Mexico managed to get an interview with the President. Earlier Senator Fall had declared on the floor of the Senate, "We have a petticoat government! Mrs. Wilson is President!" Fall had also tried to get the President proved insane, unconscious, or paralyzed—even a prisoner in the White House. So, when he called on the President, he was far from being a welcome guest. At the close of the brief interview, at which Fall had been the loser, he bent over and, as if in an effort to salvage something from the meeting, said: "Mr. President, I am praying for you." "Which way, Senator?" asked the sick but discerning President, and Fall fled the room.[2] When evil offers concern and "prayer," beware!

Evil is deceptive, stupid, bad; evil had made a mess of running the world. Satan was proposing that Christ take the nations; they would be given to him. The nations, so the devil indicated, would belong to Christ; Christ could do with them as he pleased. If he did not like the way evil was running

the world, here was his chance to govern the world as it ought
to be governed.

**But It Sounded
Good**
There is a third reason for
the appeal of this temptation:
on the surface the proposition
sounded good. The tempter was not suggesting that Christ set
up a kingdom of brute force in opposition to a kingdom of
divine love. But there was the frank recognition that evil was
then in control of the world. The devil was suggesting that
Christ be realistic enough to admit the fact and that he and
Christ join forces. In return for worship, the devil would
deliver the world to Christ. Use the kingdom of evil to set up
the kingdom of good; use Satan in the service of God; accept
the services of the world until righteousness could take over.

Satan contended that it was idealistic and visionary to take
an absolutist position. Such a position could not be maintained. Evil was present. Jesus might wish that it was not
there, but wishing would not make it so. Evil was inescapable
and powerful; it had to be reckoned with. Come to terms with
it; use it; make it your ally, the devil was saying.

"Emperors can rule men's bodies, but they cannot enlighten
and save men's souls. Prophets and saints cannot rule. You,
coming here and now, by what you are, can at last do both." [3]
So Gerald Heard imagines the tempter arguing his case.
Heaven can come to earth only when men are ruled by
physical means for spiritual ends. Always society had faced
the same dilemma: evil men managed to get power while
good men lacked it. Why not use the power of evil in the
service of goodness? After all, force had gone far in preparing
avenues for goodness to travel. It had brought the world
under one government; it had built roads that joined the
nations of that ruling power; it had cleared the sea lanes of

pirates; it had gone far toward giving the varied peoples one language. In many ways Caesar had made the world one. All this was available; evil had accomplished it; evil was ready to trade it for worship. Evil was ready to make a deal.

But making a deal or compromise goes against the grain of the idealist; he wishes neither to yield nor to bend. Satan contends, however, that you do not live in the kingdom of God—not yet; you live in the kingdom of this world now. Goodness cannot afford to ignore the need and suffering of people. If goodness is *really* goodness, it must be willing to compromise some ideals if doing so will bring wholeness and health to those in need. Doing anything less would be selfish; then goodness would itself become the thing it fights against.

"You have to sacrifice scruple: yes, for a little peace of mind for the sake of mankind and of their peace forever." Heard imagines the tempter saying: "You must love your neighbor more than you love your own matchless moral record. You must be prepared to be misunderstood, maligned, to do apparent temporary wrong. There is for you, Great Soul, only one commandment: to love man more than you love even your own highest self!" And there Christ made his decision.

"No! No! That is wrong." Heard interprets him as saying: "There you are forcing a lie upon me! There is not one commandment. There are two—man I may and must love as myself, but God and His highest law more than I love even my fellow. That must mean, it can only mean, that there are some things I cannot do even to save my neighbor." [4]

More Than One Commandment Here's truth in paradox. There are some things a man may not do even to help his neighbor. If that be treason, those who worship man will have to make the most of it. Jesus never said that the first commandment was to love man. He said the first commandment was to love God and that the *second* commandment was that man must love his neighbor as he loves himself. Man may not love his neighbor as much as he loves God; man may not love his neighbor in the place of his God; man may not love his neighbor as his God. He must love God with all his heart, his soul, his strength, and mind. Then, and only then, can he love himself intelligently. From this intelligent self-love, based upon and growing out of supreme love for God, will come his basis and standard for loving his neighbor.

The Scriptures affirm that "God is love." They do not affirm that "love is God." There is a difference; the difference is vital. Love is *of* God. It originates with him; not just our love for God but all worthy loves spring from God. But God is not the product of love, nor does he have his being in love. God is self-sustaining. We cannot love God and hate our brothers. That does not mean that when we love our brothers we necessarily love God. When a man trusts God, that man must work for God and his kingdom. But that is not to say that a man gains God by his works.

"Thou shalt have no other gods before me." The commandment stands not as an edict of a jealous tyrant but as the wisdom of a loving Father. Man may not put his neighbor before his God. Man may not put his father or his mother, his wife or children, his brothers or sisters, or even his own life, before his love of God in Christ. If he does so, he is not worthy of God's love. This is what Jesus was saying in Luke 14:33. Idolatry does not depend upon a graven image; it begins when a person lets *anything* take God's place.

None is more pitiable than the man who has loved something or someone more than he loved God. He may have loved God, but God was not first. When he lost the thing or person who had first place, the structure of life and value crashed, and from the wreckage the individual was able to salvage nothing! He was as one who was ready to "curse God and die," or he became morose and bitter, spending his life in rebellion, trying to "get even" with God.

Now, this is not just an individual matter; it concerns our human relationships as well. We do not adequately love or serve man when we make man our first love and object of service. It is only when man is placed in a secondary relationship that he can receive first-class treatment from us.

In *Hounds of Spring*, Sylvia Thompson has a serious talk with her father. It goes like this: "There isn't religion for our generation, as there use to be—I mean quite certain, helping religion that explains and alleviates a little. When you haven't any religion—well, real ideals to live for—there isn't any absolute wrong, Daddy, just small mistakes and successes." [5] Now there is a current picture for you, no "absolute wrong . . . just small mistakes and successes."

People are shoved about as pawns from the best of motives. There are no fixed stars in our firmament of human relations. We mistake pity for love, compromise for forgiveness, and desire for aspiration. Some years ago, Graham Greene shouted this truth from the house-tops in a novel called *The Heart of the Matter*. It is the story of a man who built his life on pity and compassion for the unfortunate. He did not put himself or his own welfare first; he tried to put the welfare of others first. But in Scobie, the deputy commissioner, there was no unyielding loyalty to God. Putting others before God or himself, he not only failed himself and God; he failed the very persons whom he put ahead of God and himself.

Scobie was a religious person. He believed that he could love God only by loving others. Firmly believing this, he soon arrived at the belief that love for God was a by-product of his love for his neighbor. The greater his sacrifices for his neighbor, the greater his sacrifice for God. Failing to give God his highest allegiance, he was left to his own wisdom in determining what was best for his neighbors. Instead of being responsible *under God to* his neighbors, he became *personally responsible for* his neighbors. See how it works.

Through his great love for his wife, he compromised his integrity as a police officer. He began to borrow money from a smuggler. He did this, not for selfish reasons, but for domestic reasons. He borrowed it because on his meager salary he could not satisfy his wife's expensive taste. His compassion and concern for the captain of a ship who did business with enemies of his country cause Scobie to withhold a report that he knew was his official duty to file. Through pity and compassion for an unfortunate young widow, Scobie became an adulterer. He was led into the situation because, in his confused state, he honestly believed he had an obligation to alleviate her loneliness.

In every instance, Scobie acted on the principle that his first and highest duty was to others. In every instance, what he actually did was to confuse and to injure the very persons whom he loved. The key to Scobie's tragedy came out in a letter he wrote to the lonely widow, Helen Roth: "I love you more than myself . . . more than God I think. . . . I want more than anything in the world to make you happy." Later he said to her, "I'll always come if you want me." "Will you?" she asks. "Always. If I'm alive," he replies. "God can wait, he thought." [6]

No Clear Title   In the second place, Jesus refused Satan's offer because Satan could not give a clear title to the world that he was offering. Satan said: "To you I will give all this authority; for it has been delivered to me,

and I give it to whom I will." There was an element of truth
in that statement; there usually is an *element of truth* in what
Satan says. Satan owned the Roman emperor; the emperor
owned the Roman Empire; the empire owned the world; the
empire had won the world and held it by Satan's ways and
means of power.

It is one thing to have temporary control of something, and
another thing to own it outright. It is the Judeo-Christian
faith that "the earth is the Lord's, and the fulness thereof." If
this faith be based on fact, God and God alone can give a
clear title to the earth. Man is only a trustee and will be held
responsible. Yet man in his evil pride continues to boast of
his ownership. Many centuries ago the prophet Ezekiel
taunted Pharaoh for saying, "My Nile is my own; I made it.
In an old rabbinical tale two wealthy men asked the rabbi to
settle a dispute between them over the ownership of a piece of
land. The rabbi said that he would ask the land to which it
belonged. He put his ear down to the earth and listened
closely and then said: "The earth says that it does not belong
to either of you; you belong to it. Dust thou art, and to dust
returnest." The rabbi might have added, "But the spirit
and the earth returnest to God who gave them."

In *The Universe Is My Hobby,* Dudley Zuver said that
while we were still ridiculing the American Indians for
selling Manhattan Island for a few dollars to the white man,
we had not matured enough to appreciate the Indian's position. They considered the Europeans fools for giving money
for what was no man's to sell in the first place. When Satan
promised to give the nations to Jesus in return for worship, he
was promising something that did not belong to him and,
therefore, could not be given by him to anyone with a clear
title.

Third, Jesus saw the hidden threat in Satan's proposition.

Satan said, "Worship me, and I will give you the nations." He said nothing about service. It was as if Satan had said, "It is your worship that I want; I care nothing about your service; serve anyone, anywhere, any time you will. Bow down to me in worship and rise up to whomsoever you will in service."

Jesus saw that worship and service were inextricably bound together. To worship truly means to serve. Not only will the person who truly worships Satan go out to serve Satan; in the very act of worshiping Satan, he is serving Satan. The same is true for the man who truly worships God. Too long man has sought to separate worship and service. It is impossible. It is possible, of course, for a man to go through a ritual and to perform a ceremony, call that worship of God, and then go out to serve the devil. But that is something quite different from what the New Testament means by worship.

"The test of worship," says Bishop John A. T. Robinson, "is how far it makes us *more sensitive* to 'the beyond in our midst,' to the Christ in the hungry, the naked, the homeless, and the prisoner. Only if we are *more likely* to recognize him there after attending an act of worship is that worship Christian rather than a piece of religiosity in Christian dress." [7]

What the young in heart can see may be hid from the veteran. For sin is unique in this: the more experience a man has in it, the less he knows about it. The young knight who has kept his body strong and his mind clear is far more sensitive to the dangers of alcohol than the drunk on skid row with bleary eyes and an appetite that makes him glad to sell his soul for another drink. The virgin with holy dreams of worthy motherhood is far more shocked at debased use of the God-given wonder of sex than the woman who has known a multitude of men who have loved her for the gratification of their lust, but never one who loved her for herself.

Let the old and the tired and the experienced compromiser smile his knowing smiles and in his worldly wisdom say to the young idealist, "Yes, I can understand; for when I was your age I felt and thought just as you do." The young idealist might reply, "My greatest fear is that when 1 am your age I shall think and feel as you do." Dorothy Parker has a penetrating and disturbing little poem called "The Veteran," in which she says:

> When I was young and bold and strong,
> Oh, right was right, and wrong was wrong!
> My plume on high, my flag unfurled,
> I rode away to right the world.
> "Come out, you dogs, and fight!" said I,
> And wept there was but once to die.
>
> But I am old; and good and bad
> Are woven in a crazy plaid.
> I sit and say, "The world is so;
> And he is wise who lets it go.
> A battle lost, a battle won—
> The difference is small, my son."
>
> Inertia rides and riddles me;
> The which is called Philosophy.[8]

O Christ of the true eye, the clear mind, and the pure heart, how true that is! Archbishop Soderblom once said, "The strength of our Saviour was that he never became accustomed to wrong."

Ruined World for Satan   Once more, Christ refused to yield to the temptation because he knew he could ruin the heart of the world for Satan. No matter to whom Satan gives the world, even on a temporary basis, some men will insist on saying, "Thou shalt worship the Lord thy God, and him only shalt thou serve." We may continue to have tyrants who blow their horns, rattle their sabers, and test their nuclear explosives; but the hearts of men will continue to long for more than the tyrant can give. They will seek, in Chesterton's words, for an older place than Eden and a taller town than Rome.

Men may refuse to give God his rightful place in their hearts, but Christ has ruined the heart of the world for any other Lord. Men can never be content in the worship of evil. Robert Jeffers, the poet, was the son of a professor in a theological seminary. The poet grew up in a home of faith. He was once described as one of the "sons of talent born in the church who have departed from the family faith in our time, yet always with some remaining indebtedness and distress." He could not elude a silent influence from his past.

In his wilderness ordeal Jesus successfully resisted all three of the tempter's propositions. He refused to take the short-cuts to win the allegiance of men. What was left? What way would Jesus choose for reaching the hearts of men? He chose the way of consecration, the way of humble service, the way of mediation between God and man, the way of love and reconciliation. In the synagogue of Nazareth he declared:

> The Spirit of the Lord is upon me,
> because he has anointed me to preach good news to
>   the poor.
> He has sent me to proclaim release to the captives
> and recovering of sight to the blind,
> to set at liberty those who are oppressed,
> to proclaim the acceptable year of the Lord.[9]

Today we observe that choice from the distance of two thousand years. How does it seem? We certainly do not see all things put under his feet. We do see Jesus. His name, his character, his life, his love, and his choice stand out more clearly to be desired than ever on that day when he turned from the offer of evil in the desert and chose the way of consecration in the service of mankind. The constructive and creative forces of this world have followed his lead.

The great and the good and the helpful from all lands and peoples and tongues and classes have come laying their trophies at his feet. Listen to F. W. Boreham on the sixtieth anniversary of his entrance into the ministry and seriously ask if they do not voice your own earnest desire:

From the day I was ordained to this day, the one passionate desire of my heart has been to lead my hearers to Christ. I have never entered a pulpit without the feeling that, if only the people could catch a vision of the Saviour, they would have no alternative but to lay their devotion at his feet. My soul has caught fire whenever I have exalted the Cross. I have never in my life been so perfectly happy as when preaching on such texts as "God so loved the world," . . . "The Son of Man is come to seek and to save that which was lost." [10]

Ahead, the way seems long and the night is dark, so dark that cats might run into each other! Will the way of Christ work? Eternity and time, history and experience, faith and life say yes. One other thing is equally sure; nothing else will work. Does the way of Jesus have your vote?

> What is the final ending?
> The issue, can we know?
>
> .   .   .   .
>
> This is our faith tremendous,
> Our wild hope, who shall scorn,
> That in the name of Jesus
> The world shall be reborn! [11]

6

"The Time Has Come at Last"

MARK 1:14–15

William Lyon Phelps, greatly loved professor of English literature at Yale University and an ordained Baptist minister, had his summer home at Huron City in the state of Michigan. For many years he preached to an overflow crowd each summer while at Huron City.

The service was held at three o'clock in the afternoon, an hour that did not conflict with any other service of worship and an hour that no one else wanted. The meeting was held in a Methodist church; the preacher was Baptist; many denominations were represented, including Roman Catholics, Christian Scientists, Methodists, Presbyterians, Baptists, Congregationalists, Mormons, Jews, and Unitarians.

Often Dr. Phelps was asked, "What do you say to such a collection of sects? Do you give a literary lecture or a moral talk?" His answer was always the same, namely that he preached only the gospel. He said: "No subject is more interesting than religion; the trouble with many ministers is that they preach everything except religion, and wonder why their audiences diminish." And again, "I remember an earnest Protestant pastor (now with God) who conceived it his duty during an entire Presidential campaign to preach against one of the candidates; the trouble with any minister who has only one idea is that his flock knows what he is going to say; they lose interest and stay away. And this man kept it up; after the candidate whom he had opposed was elected, and he with other men at a club was listening to the election returns, he cried out in distress of mind, "Oh, what shall I do now?" Professor Lounsbury (also of Yale faculty) remarked, "There is only one thing, Doctor, for you to do now; and that is, preach the gospel!" [1]

Jesus Came Preaching

"Now after that John was put in prison, Jesus came into Galilee, preaching the gospel of the kingdom of God." The sentence is heavy with significance. Jesus of Nazareth, owned and approved of God at his baptism, came at a definite time to a definite place doing a specific thing in history. His coming at that time and place took into account current conditions.

It was after John had been put in prison that Jesus came into Galilee. Some people claim that Jesus went to Galilee because it was safer there. If he had remained in Judea, he might have faced the same danger from Herod that John had experienced. So Jesus retired to Galilee. His time of death had not arrived; he had things to do before hazarding his life.

This is a possible view, but it is not the only possible view. Galilee was no retreat! Galilee could be dangerous. Judea kept a close watch on Galilee. The Galileans were independent, freedom-loving, and were ready to rebel on the slightest provocation. Jesus could get a great hearing there. It was his home territory; he knew the people and the area. John had announced him; John had been courageous and loyal; through this courage and loyalty, John had been imprisoned. It was time for Jesus to honor the word of John, as well as the time of God. Jesus was not seeking to evade Herod; through honoring the divine "fulness of time" and the prison experience of John, he was saying, as he would say again later, "Go tell that fox [Herod], Behold I cast out devils, and I do cures today and tomorrow!"

"Jesus came into Galilee preaching." Why did he come "preaching"? Why did he not come writing, gathering an army, running a political campaign, stirring up a revolution? We may well wonder whether Satan did not tempt him again at this point. Why not let the imprisonment of John be the spark that would set off the explosion of rebellion? Release John; overpower the garrisons of Rome; set up a government of the people and for the people? Satan had tempted him before. Could he have tried it again? We know only that Jesus came preaching.

This was the means he chose. John called him "the Word." Jesus trusted the spoken word; he trusted the hearing ear. He believed it was possible to communicate the message of the love of God through the preached word. It is interesting to note that Jesus not only began his ministry with the spoken word; he closed his earthly mission still relying upon the spoken word. Let every honest preacher take heart! Let him believe in his message, and let him believe in his method. Let him believe so much in both that the message may master the preacher, and the preacher master the method. Both are necessary. On one occasion a deacon commenting on his new pastor said, "Our young man has settled a lot of problems we never heard of and answered a lot of questions nobody was asking."

"Jesus came into Galilee, preaching the gospel of the kingdom of God, and saying, The time is fulfilled, and the kingdom of God is at hand: repent ye, and believe the gospel." It has been said that every great new idea has had its own watchword. A leader needs to be able to put his message

into an impressive sentence or slogan that the people can
grasp and understand with their minds and treasure in their
hearts. For Jesus, such a word was "kingdom of God," or
"kingdom of heaven."

The idea had a long history in Jewish thought. Jesus
changed the concept but kept the form. For Jesus, the kingdom of God was in the heart, and it was in the world. It was a
matter of sovereignty, but that sovereignty was not geograph-
ical. It was not over acres and miles as much as it was over
hearts and wills. The kingdom of God was where God ruled.
Once Count Leo Tolstoi remonstrated with an enthusiastic
student: "You sweat too much blood for the world. If
you want to make the world better, you have to be the
best you can. . . . You cannot bring the kingdom of God
into the world until you bring it into your own heart
first." Jesus said his kingdom was not of this world; therefore,
his followers did not fight for it. The kingdom was past,
present, and future. It had come in part; it was being offered
in the present; its full acceptance and realization were to
come in the future. Men entered this kingdom through a
childlike faith, a forgiving spirit, a sincere trust, and a demon-
stration of the love of God—agape—toward others.

Few men have given a more beautiful and poignant expression of the kingdom of God than Charles Rann Kennedy in
his fine play *The Terrible Meek*. Its setting is Calvary after
the crucifixion. Standing at the base of the cross is Mary, the
mother of Jesus. The Roman centurion speaks:

I tell you, woman, this dead son of yours, disfigured, shamed,
spat upon, has built a kingdom this day that can never die. The
living glory of him rules it. . . . He and his brothers have been
moulding and making it through the long ages: they are the only
ones who ever really did possess it: not the proud: not the idle,
not the wealthy, not the vaunting empires of the world. Some-

thing has happened up here on this hill to-day to shake all our kingdoms of blood and fear to the dust. The earth is his, the earth is theirs, and they made it. The meek, the terrible meek, the fierce agonizing meek are about to enter into their inheritance.[2]

Good News! Jesus came into Galilee
About God preaching the gospel, the good news about God. The word "gospel" came close to summarizing the entire message of Jesus. The opening verse of Mark begins: "The beginning of the gospel of Jesus Christ." The word appears seventy-two times in the New Testament. The kingdom which Jesus proclaimed was "good news." For all of John's greatness, his message was "bad news." He talked about consuming fires, winnowing fans, an ax that was laid at the root of the tree.

When James S. Pike was United States Minister to the Netherlands in 1863, he visited Thomas Carlyle. Pike came away from the visit shaking his head and saying that Carlyle seemed to believe there was a God, but that the devil was more than a match for him. Whatever may have been Carlyle's view, and Pike's words are not an adequate evaluation of the philosophy of the great Scot, certainly Jesus had no such conviction. He preached a message of good news. T. S. Eliot comes near the message of Jesus in these words:

There shall always be the Church and the World
And the Heart of Man
Shivering and fluttering between, choosing and the chosen,
Valiant, ignoble, dark and full of light
Swinging between Hell Gate and Heaven Gate.
And the Gates of Hell shall not prevail.
Darkness now, then
Light,
Light![3]

The content of the New Testament word for gospel, the good news, is rich and full. In a world of lies, the gospel is the good news of truth; Paul would not yield to the Judaizers for he wanted the "truth of the gospel" to continue with the Galatians. In a world that has lost its nerve, the gospel is the good news of hope; Paul cautioned the Colossians not to turn from the "hope of the gospel" which had been preached to them and to others. In a world of threats and demands, the gospel is the good news of gift and promise; the Ephesians were reminded that they were partakers of God's promise in Christ by the gospel. In a world of strife, the gospel is the good news of peace. In a world of lost men and women, the gospel is the good news of salvation; the apostle reminded the Ephesians that they had trusted in the gospel of their salvation. In a world of skepticism, the gospel comes as the good news of the risen Christ affirmed in the gospel Paul preached. The gospel is the good news of immortality.

> Nothing but blackness above
> And nothing that moves but the cars. . . .
> God, if You wish for our love,
> Fling us a handful of stars! [4]

The gospel is the good news of God. This was news, and it was good. The pagan gods were vengeful and vindictive and jealous. Much that the Jews had been taught of the God of the Old Testament had emphasized his wrath, anger, threats, and jealousy. Jesus did not deny the holiness, righteousness, and judgment of God, but he preached the good news that God is a loving Father. The gospel is the good news of God not only because God is good, but also because God sent it. God took the initiative. This calls for gratitude and humility. Charles W. Eliot, famous Harvard president, once wrote to a friend: "I notice in a good many young men that their religion seems to consist in a burning desire to be of service to those they live with and to their own community, but I cannot help thinking that 'to walk humbly with thy God' is a very important part of religion."

The gospel is also spoken of as the good news of Jesus Christ. It is the good news of Christ in two ways. It came to men through Christ; without him we would not have it. It is the good news of Christ in that he embodied it; without him we would never have seen it lived out among us. He did not just come saying, "There it is, accept it." He came and his life said: "Here it is; this is what it is; this is how one acts and reacts when he incarnates it."

This embodying of the gospel by Christ did more to impress and challenge men than words alone could ever do. Men looked at him, and they knew how to evaluate; they watched him, and they knew what their relationship to others should be. When they heard him pray, they knew how spiritually poverty stricken they were. Perceiving his courage and boldness, they sought to imitate him. Seeing him forgive, they wanted to be like him. When they failed and embarrassed his cause, he loved them still; and they were inspired to love others even in the face of disappointment. So they were emboldened to accept his invitation and follow his example, no matter how poorly they might do.

Carl Sandburg used to say, after he had published his *Chicago Poems,* that there was one vast difference between him, Dante, and Milton. While Dante and Milton wrote about hell and had never seen the place, he wrote about Chicago after having looked the town over rather carefully for many years! In a very real sense, something of the same might be said for those who came before the day of Jesus, or those who have come since but have never known his spirit and message. These may write and talk about the gospel, never

having seen it embodied in life; only those who experience
Christ have firsthand information.

This good news that was central in the life and message of
Jesus was not a human discovery; it was a divine disclosure.
We have a saying, "Too good to be true," but of the gospel it
is far more reasonable to say, "Too good not to be true." Still,
the truth of the gospel is so different from anything that man
knows in the natural world that he finds it difficult to believe.
In trade, labor negotiations, and other human dealings, men
almost uniformly act upon the assumption that everyone has
an "angle"; everyone is out to see what he can get out of
another. We automatically wonder, "What's in it for him?"
or "What do I get out of it?" or "What is the payoff?"

When you face the good news of God in Christ, all that is
reversed. The gospel comes with gifts; it is grace—marvelous
grace. It comes with a program in which everything is based
upon "unmerited favor." It is not based upon what God can
get out of your life, but rather what your life will accept and
use from the bounty of God. No wonder God had to reveal it
to men; even when he did, men found it—still find it—hard
to believe and to accept. Paul said, "I certify you, brethren,
that the gospel which was preached of me is not after man. For
I neither received it of man, neither was I taught it, but by
the revelation of Jesus Christ" (Gal. 1:11–12). The gospel
reverses the ways of the world. Peter Taylor Forsyth said that
"Christ came not to be ministered to, but to minister; and
our first duty, therefore, is to be ministered to by him."

Repentance
and Acceptance
In Christ, the good news is
the motive for repentance. Of
course, the necessity for re-
pentance was an integral part of the message of Christ. Both
John and Jesus called for a radical change in the thinking and

acting of men. John called on the people to repent because
God's wrath was about to be released. The kingdom was at
hand, and the people had better square their lives with the
commandments of God; for the wicked would be like chaff
which the wind drives away or like a tree cut down by a sharp
ax. He warned the people "to flee from the wrath to come."
Repent; make straight your lives; God will require an ac-
counting; you cannot escape.

Jesus said, "The time is fulfilled, and the kingdom of God
is at hand: repent ye, and believe the gospel." What a
difference! The kingdom of God is at hand. The time that
you and your predecessors have waited for so long has finally
arrived. God is ready to assume the control of human hearts
and wills. Satan has had that control long enough; now God
will take over. This is great good news. Repent that you may
be ready for this wonderful thing that God will do. "Believe
the gospel!" Believe this good news!

It is possible to make too wide a gap between Jesus and
John. Jesus required repentance; John welcomed the righteousness of God. John certainly did not have a higher ethical
and moral standard for those who would welcome Christ than
Christ himself required. Both saw the sinfulness of man and
the righteousness of God. Both Jesus and John knew that
fundamental changes in men were essential.

Some years ago a group of scientists were carrying out in-
vestigations at the South Pole. In their workroom was a large
globe of the world. The globe was upside down. They found
that when they were right side up at the South Pole, the world
seemed upside down. That is the case when we face Jesus. We
come to him standing upright in our own eyes, and we find
that we are wrong side up in his sight. Only when our own
motives, plans, purposes, and drives are turned upside down
are they right side up with him.

Professor C. E. M. Joad once said, "The world has a long way to go before its practice squares with its professions, but the first step is for the profession to condemn its practices, and that step it has taken." Let the church confess its failures; let it profess its Christ and his way of life. By no stretch of honesty can we believe, personally or as groups of Christians, that we measure up to the Christian ideal for life and living. In selfishness and greed, in appetite and sex, in race and prejudice, in crime and punishment, the honest man must repent.

We have done those things that we ought not to have done, and we have left undone those things that ought to have been done. We have not done unto others as we would have them do unto us. We have not gone the second mile, nor turned the other cheek, nor sought first the kingdom of God and his righteousness. We have shown respect to persons. The color of a man's skin rather than the integrity of his heart has weighted our scales. We are good at rationalizing and analyzing. We question a man's motives, but the sharpness of our questioning depends more upon his status and color than it does upon his record. How many white persons who join our churches would ever make it if we demanded completely pure motives?

Professor Joad said that the first thing for the church to do was to "condemn its practices." And he said that the church had taken the step in that direction. To no small extent that is true. Many Christians have cried out with Isaiah: "Woe is me! for I am undone; . . . I am a man of unclean lips, and I dwell in the midst of a people of unclean lips." Modern writers, too, confess the failures of the church.

Paradoxical as it may seem, however, this can be a deadly emotion as well as a life-giving one. We can condemn our practices until we feel hopelessly guilty. We can confess the failures of our churches until we come to feel that there is no good thing in them, that God is gone from these dead skeletons. It does no good for an individual or an institution to wallow in guilt; it can be definitely harmful. St. Theresa wisely said: "It is a great grace of God to practice self-examination, but too much is as bad as too little. Believe me, by God's help, we shall advance more by contemplating the Divinity than keeping our eyes fixed on ourselves, poor creatures of earth that we are."

The point that is emphasized is just this: we must go beyond repentance to belief in the good news. Jesus said: "Repent ye, *and believe the gospel*." The prodigal son confessed and repented; he also believed and acted on that belief. He walked out of the pigpen and back to his father's house. No amount of repentance alone would have solved his problem; he had to believe in his father's love and be willing to accept it. True, it was necessary for him to repent, or he would not have headed back home. Yet, he might have wallowed in guilt and self-pity until both the pigs and the cows came home and still remained in the barnyard! Some people make a profession of repenting! They feel good because they feel so guilty; they get their "kicks" from feeling so "kickless." They try to substitute repentance for belief and faith.

This is no way to honor the God and Father of our Lord Jesus Christ. This is, rather, the way to discredit him, to act like he is a tyrant who enjoys seeing his subjects cringe and cower before him. The Pope in *The Shoes of the Fisherman* says: "The good shepherd seeks out the lost sheep and carries them home on his shoulder. He does not demand that they come crawling back, draggle-tailed and remorseful." [5] Certainly the good shepherd takes no delight in seeing the sheep substitute self-rejection for belief in the good news of God.

Let us have faith in the forgiving grace of God rather than in our sins and failures. Let us dare to believe that God in Christ is great enough to forgive our sin and powerful enough to make even our weakness serve him. The "Rug of Ardebil" hangs in the British Museum. It is considered to be the finest rug in the world. The story of its creation is inspiring. Maksoud of Ardebil was a poor weaver of Persia during the sixteenth century. His humble task was to sweep the mosque in return for his daily bread. As he was sweeping the mosque one day, he saw the light of the sun streaming through its dome. He was impressed with the intricate mosaic on the floor created by these rays. Suddenly, a great desire overwhelmed him; he would weave a rug to capture in color and texture the pattern created by the rays of the sun streaming through the dome. With only a rude hand loom, he went to work. But through years of dedication, patience, and skill he created the finest rug in the world.

Meant For All Men   The good news of God is meant for all men. The Jews had always believed, as William Barclay says, that in God's economy there was a "most favored nation clause." God's promises were for the Jews as they were not to and for others. Since Abraham was their father, they were God's favorites. Nothing in the teachings of Jesus leaves the Jews out of the good news, but all other people are included, too. In foretelling the destruction of Jerusalem and the persecution of his followers, Jesus said that the gospel had first to be preached to all nations. When Paul was being questioned in Jerusalem, Peter said that God had decided that the Gentiles—all people other than Jews— should hear the gospel.

In the words of the lovely and reverent spiritual, "he's got the whole world in his hand." There is good scriptural basis for that song, too. The Hebrew prophets declared that nations afar shall come and worship God. Pagan peoples were seen as Israel to God. The psalmist was sure that he could never go any where that the hand of the Lord would not lead and hold him. He heard God saying: "The world is mine." Not only has he got the whole world in his hand; he's got it in his heart.

Some years ago, my family and I visited Concord, Massachusetts. On a red-letter day, I went down to Walden Pond and found the spot where Henry David Thoreau built his small cabin. In his famous book, *Walden,* Thoreau says that there in his cabin he had three chairs, "one for solitude, two for friendship, three for society." He who would hear the good news must have these chairs. He must in the deep solitude of his own individual soul accept or reject that good news. His close friends, his family, his neighbors must be influenced by this good news. But society at large, the "whole world" that the spiritual sings about, must also hear of this good news.

This leads to another great truth about the good news: the good news was not only *meant* for all men, but all who have heard it must share it with others. When a man hears and accepts the good news, he becomes a trustee or steward, of the good news. He is throughout life a partner with God in declaring the gospel.

Carl Sandburg says that the War Between the States was fought over a verb. In addressing the New School in New York City on April 6, 1959, he referred to Governor Faubus and the then tense racial situation in Little Rock, Arkansas. Sandburg said that Mr. Faubus would not understand much that Lincoln said. For example, he did not understand that that fearful four-year bloodbath of the 1860's had one curious result. Before that war the Department of State in treaties with foreign nations wrote, "The United States *are*," but after the war it was written, "The United States *is*." "The war was fought over a verb." [6]

In like manner, the church of Jesus Christ moves out into the battle of life for one purpose: to lead all those who know Christ to share the good news with all those who know him not. The end result will be: "The kingdoms of this world are become the kingdoms of our Lord, and his Christ." No longer two kingdoms and, therefore, to be written with an *are*, but one kingdom to be written with an *is!*

A man is never too humble nor does he rise to such greatness that this privilege and responsibility do not abide. Bishop Gerald Kennedy says that he is the only Methodist bishop to flunk a college course in Bible. When he was elected bishop, he had a letter from his old teacher congratulating him but adding, "You still owe me a paper on Jeremiah." The obligation remains.

No chapters in the annals of heroism are more thrilling than those which tell of men who have gladly claimed the privilege and joyfully discharged the duty of telling the good news to others. None excelled the circuit-riding preachers on our own western frontier:

[They were] ready to go anywhere, at any time, where sinners were in need of the saving word. No settlement was too run-down, too remote for them. They roughed it along the trails in snow and rain, taking their chances on bears, wolves, cutthroats and Indians. They put up where they could find local hospitality, which usually meant cornbread and pork and a spot for sleeping on the dirt floor by the fire. They spent a good part of their lives hungry, wet, cold, verminous and saddlesore; and if they did not die young of consumption, they could expect an old age of rheumatism and dyspepsia. But they went almost literally everywhere.[7]

Luke says that when Mary and Joseph presented the child, Jesus, in the Temple for dedication, a just and devout man named Simeon was there "waiting for the consolation of Israel." Not only was Simeon waiting, but also Israel and the whole world were waiting for that. The world is still waiting in all those places and parts where God's love has not been declared and lived and believed. This good news is the consolation of all men. For the gospel of Christ "is the power of God unto salvation to every one that believeth."

7

"Come with Me, and I Will Make You"

MARK 1:16–20

During the "silent years" in Nazareth, Jesus had faithfully served and patiently waited. At his baptism he had committed himself and received his Father's approval. In the wilderness of temptation he had forged his ways and means. Immediately following the temptation experiences, he had announced himself and his program. It was now time to select and mobilize his men.

In *The Making of the President, 1960,* Theodore H. White tells of a significant meeting that took place in the Harvard Club on Boston's Commonwealth Avenue. The time was an evening in January of 1960. The personalities were young John F. Kennedy, then Senator Kennedy, and a group of his former professors from Harvard University. Over the past eight years, young Kennedy had been calling on these men for ideas, information, and analysis. On that evening in January he faced them in the Harvard Club and bluntly told them that they were now mobilized. He said that if there were Stevensonians in the group who wished to leave, they might do so. All who stayed would be a part of that mobilized unit. He and that mobilized unit were moving out; their object was the Presidency of the United States.[1]

A leader may be committed himself, committed to the right ideas and to the right person; his area of operations may be decided upon; the time of his attack may be pinpointed; but he must still rely upon his men. He must have around him those upon whom he can rely, men who will accept and carry out his orders and his plans.

Douglas Blatherwick records an incident that took place years ago at a great concert given by the Halle Orchestra under the skilled direction of Sir John Barbirolli. The hall was packed; every seat was taken. As the crowd was dispersing, a church member spotted his minister and said, "Tell me, when are we going to have an auditorium packed on a Sunday evening as this place was packed this evening." The minister answered, "When, like Sir John Barbirolli, I have under me eighty trained and disciplined men." [2] Both leadership and "followship" are essential; neither may be discounted.

Why He Needed Help

Professor William Barclay says that Jesus chose his men because he wanted his work to go *on* and because he wanted his work to go *out*. I would add a third reason: he needed them because he wanted his work to go *in*. Consider those three dimensions. Jesus wanted his work to go on. If that was to be accomplished in the plan and providence of God, he had to have assistance. It seems quite definite that from the very beginning, Jesus knew an early death awaited him. Early or late, by violent or natural means, his own personal human leadership would come to an end. If his work was to go on, there would have to be a nucleus of men who knew him, were committed to him, and were dedicated to work for that for which he would give his life; otherwise his work would die with him.

The latest statistics list the Christian population of the

world at 916,400,000. What stands between that figure and the total extinction of Christianity? Just one generation, that is all. If the Christian population of the world is to "remain steady," 916,400,000 persons must, in one way or another, become identified with Christianity during the next generation. Even that does not take in normal losses. If the Christian population is to increase in numbers, there will have to be more—many more—than the present figure affiliating during the next generation. This serves to point up the necessity for the work and word of Jesus to go on and to go out.

In the days of his flesh, Jesus was limited in time and in place like other men. If he was in Galilee, he could not be in Jerusalem; if he was in Samaria, he could not be in the region of Tyre and Sidon at the same time. There was no means of mass communication; his voice could be heard by only a few thousands at once. His message had to be taken by men, by word of mouth. This was the way messages were taken; it was expected that messages would be taken this way. He told his men that they were to be his messengers; they were to bear witness of him; "and as you go, say" were his instructions.

Here is seen the evangelistic nature of the church. Truman Douglass once said that many people were so busy doing church work that they had no time to do the work of the church. Basic and central to the work of the church is evangelism, bearing witness, passing on the torch—the light of the world. This work of evangelism may be, will be, done differently by different groups. It will be done differently by the same group in different times and different places. But if the work of Jesus is to go on and to go out, men must tell the story.

Elizabeth O'Connor illustrates this in her story of the Church of the Saviour in Washington, D. C. entitled *Call to*

Commitment. She shares with her readers the dream that Gordon Cosby, the pastor, had during his days as a chaplain in World War II. Cosby knew the kind of church he wanted to sponsor and to pastor. It was to be a church for the classes *and* the masses, a church for the races and the nations, the colors and the cultures. Evangelism was basic in his thinking. In one letter home, he explained that if each member were really committed and won two other persons to Christ each year, and always two won two, within twenty-five years the whole world would be won to the Saviour. Sheets of statistics were enclosed in the letter to substantiate his statement. Gordon Cosby came home; the church was organized. Many of the original ideas were incorporated. Fourteen years later Elizabeth O'Connor wrote:

We still thought then that two would win two and that in twenty-five years the world would be converted and the kingdom of God be established here on earth. We probably would not have stated it quite so naively, but in our hearts this is what we believed. It seemed that the Good News would be easy to tell, and who hearing would not respond? Now, fourteen years later, we know that it does not come about in this way. We know a little bit more of what it costs to save another life. We know the years of nurture required to make a mature Christian and we know that the days cry out for this.[3]

Let two comments be made on that statement. First, we must be grateful that such an ideal and such a dream existed. Second, while the timetable may have to be revised because of additional experience, never let it be doubted that the evangelistic impulse felt so strongly in the early days must remain a central concern of every Christian church.

Jesus needed followers, helpers, because he wanted his work to go in—into the hearts and wills of the people. If this is to be done, the people must participate in the venture themselves. They must become involved. The work must be their work. Evangelism is not only necessary for a lost world, it is also necessary to a saved church. As the church bears witness to its Lord, its Lord becomes real to the church. As the individual tells others of what Christ can do, Christ does for the one who bears the witness. It was "as they went" that the lepers were healed. The Great Commission says, "Go ye into all the world and make disciples." It then adds, "Lo, I am with you." Without the "going," there would be no "remaining with"?

The great doctrine of the priesthood of all believers does not emphasize only that every man may go directly to God for himself. That is a basic part, a blessed part, of the truth. Another truth in the teaching, however, is that every believer who encounters God through Christ becomes a witness to and for the Christ whose grace has redeemed the messenger.

The Kind of Men He Wanted

The job a man has to do determines the type of men he will choose to help him to do the job. Look at the Master's men. They were young men. When Jesus walked by the seashore and called James and John, they left their father, Zebedee, in the boat and followed him. That is significant. Jesus got two men; one man was left. Did James and John come because he called them, and did Zebedee remain because he was not called? There is probably more involved than that. It is more likely that Jesus did not call Zebedee because he knew that Zebedee would not come! "Age," says Walter Russell Bowie: "did not follow him as readily as youth. There was something about him which drew the eager and adventurous, and left settled conservative people shaking their heads." [4] It is an old story. Terah dies in

Haran; Abram, his son, moves out, following the voice of God, and goes into a land he knows not of. In the first Christian sermon following the ascension of Jesus, Peter talked about young men seeing visions.

"Christianity began as young people's movement," says James S. Stewart. "Most of the Apostles were probably still in their twenties when they went out after Jesus." For proof of that, remember that when Paul wrote, almost a generation later, he said that of the five hundred to whom Christ appeared, most of them were still alive. Does it not suggest that the spiritual appeal of Jesus was mainly to the young? Again and again, Jesus addressed his disciples as "children" or "my dear children" or as Moffatt and Phillips translate the word, "lads." When the Christians drew the likeness of Jesus, as the eyes of their hearts gave them to draw it on the walls of the catacombs, they drew him "as a young shepherd out on the hills of the morning."

When we study the story of the first Twelve, it is a young man's adventure we are studying. We see them following their Leader out into the unknown, not knowing very clearly who He is, or why they are doing it, or where He is likely to lead them; but just magnetized by Him, fascinated and gripped and held by something irresistible in the Soul of Him, laughed at by friends, plotted against by foes, with doubts sometimes growing clamorous in their hearts, until they almost wished they were well out of the whole business; but still clinging to Him, coming through the ruin of their hopes to a better loyalty, and earning triumphantly at last the great name the "Te Deum" gives them, "The glorious company of the Apostles." It is worth watching them, for we may catch the infection of their spirit, and fall into step with Jesus.[5]

They were young men, and they were normal men. That is, there was nothing extraordinary about them. They were not college bred; they were not of the landed gentry; they were neither prophets nor sons of prophets. These first men were fishermen, following an honest but humble trade. They behaved much like other men behaved. They had their full quota of pride and prejudice. They were not especially brave; they were quite ambitious, though not always very intelligent about it. They quarreled often; they knew discouragement. They were individualists; no one of them was a carbon copy of another.

James and John were boisterous as thunderstorms. Peter was quick like mercury and as hard to hold; he was hot-tempered, and yet he had sharp insight and great enthusiasm. Andrew was quiet and retiring, yet constantly on the lookout for bringing people into relationship with Jesus. Matthew was a close and accurate observer. Thomas always had to contend with his doubts as if they were a "swarm of gnats"; however, once he was convinced, no one of the disciples was ready to lay more upon the line. There was a Zealot in the crowd, Simon. He had a hot heart inclined to impatience and rebellion. Each was different; each was an individualist. Jesus chose them with this in mind for "he knew what was in man." He knew that his cause would profit from unity in diversity.

These men were capable of great loyalty; they were not ashamed of enthusiasm; they were idealists. They were neither afraid to be the first to try the new nor anxious to be the last to lay the old aside. They could, would, did do a daft thing, like giving up a safe living and a comfortable home life to go traipsing off after a Dreamer who had not where to lay his head. They did not know much about this Nazarene; they knew less about his intent. They could not have passed any kind of entrance examination for a theological seminary.

Jesus accepted them on this basis. They responded to him;

they were willing to follow him; they were willing to pay something for that following. Jesus seemed to be satisfied with that. They were known as "disciples," that is, pupils or learners. They were willing to accept Jesus as their teacher; he was willing to accept them as his students. He would teach; they would learn. They were willing to give high loyalty; he was willing to give great love and fidelity. That is how it all began.

Biographers say that Hannibal won his battles not only on the field of battle but in conference with his men the day before. He would convince them that he knew his business, that he knew and had confidence in his men, and that he had the best possible plan. In his skilful counseling, he would encourage the fearful and caution the overconfident. He started where his men were, and he led them step by step to where he was. They knew that he could see it all through their eyes; but before he was through, and even before they knew it, they were seeing it through his eyes. So they went into battle as one man, seeing, acting, feeling as one with their general.

How He Called Them

Now consider how Jesus called his men. It begins with a very harmless looking statement in the first chapter of the Gospel of Mark:

Passing along by the Sea of Galilee, he saw Simon and Andrew the brother of Simon casting a net in the sea; for they were fishermen. And Jesus said to them, "Follow me and I will make you become fishers of men.". . . Going on a little farther, he saw James the son of Zebedee and John his brother, who were in their boat mending the nets. And immediately he called them; and they left their father Zebedee in the boat with the hired servants, and followed him.[6]

It all looks simple enough, or dramatic enough, depending upon your desire. Was it the first time he had seen these men? It is doubtful. Had they heard him preach? Were they friends? Had they talked about this possibility before? We do not know. There is suggested here an idea that needs to receive high priority on the list of requirements for any great leader. "He saw Simon and Andrew . . . he saw James . . . and John."

Are you impatient and feel like saying, "Oh, of course, he saw them! Otherwise, how would he be able to call?" Yes, but in the light of what we know from our vantage point, we may believe that more is involved than that. He *saw* them. He saw who they were and what they were and what they were doing and how they were doing it. He saw who they could become and what they could do and how they could become, do, and be—all this by his help. We have an expression that just about sums it up; we sometimes say of a very discerning person, "He sees right through you!" Jesus did that and more; he saw beyond them.

In writing of this passage once, Halford Luccock said that Jesus had X-ray eyes. The kind of eyes, or sight, that people have is tremendously important. There are men who have Midas eyes. Like the old fellow at whose touch everything turned to gold, these men see only gold or its equivalent whenever they look at anything or anyone. This item, this deal, this contract, this sale means so much cash in the till or collateral papers in the vault. Others have the eyes of a political climber. Everything and everyone represents so much advancement, so many votes. They do not run for office once every four years; they are always running. They never meet a person, make a contact, write a letter or an article, or attend a meeting or convention but the restless eye of the politician is loose and roving. Then there is the individual who has the lustful eye. His eye undresses every woman he sees. His sexual imagination will bridle at nothing.

Goodspeed translates Mark 11:11 as saying, "He came . . . into the Temple, and *looked it all over.*" His eyes made a very careful survey. Nothing escaped his gaze. He laid present facts along beside original intent; and when the Temple was weighed in those balances, it was found wanting. He saw it was meant to be a house of prayer for all nations, but it had been made into a den of thieves. No amount of reasoning, arguing, and rationalization could alter that fact. The distance between what that "church" was and what it was originally intended to be was a "long sea mile"!

In writing to the Colossians, Paul said, "We are asking God that you may see things, as it were, from his point of view." This was the view in which James and John, Peter and Andrew, and the others were seen when they were called. From the point of view of the school, they never would have been called. If examined by the official religious leaders, they never would have been called. From the point of view of the social register, they never would have been called. Jesus was not seeing them from any of these view-points; he was seeing them from God's point of view.

The call of Jesus involved a careful look, the look of God. It also involved an invitation. Mark says that he called to him those whom he desired. Two points may be observed here. He did the calling; he took the initiative. He always does. Later he was to remind them that he had chosen them; they had not chosen him. Jesus needed men for the most important assignment earth had ever known; he went out looking for those men. He found them, and he invited them to join him. This, of course, was a complement to these men. With all the world before him from which to choose, Jesus chose these.

So far as we know, the first twelve he invited, accepted. If this was the case, there was not a second choice in the lot. Later there would be those, like the rich young ruler, who would turn from his invitation. But these men did not. There is also the idea of a summons in the call. In Luke's version of the call, the word definitely implies a summons. So, while the call was an invitation and suggested a great compliment, it was also a rallying call—not to ease but to a cross.

As was said, these disciples did not know a great deal about Christ nor what was involved in his invitation. They simply knew that there was something about Jesus—his bearing, his voice, his spirit—that made them want to do what he invited them to do. Later they were to understand more fully what was involved. At that time, however, they were ready to risk all in loyalty to him. Look over life's prizes, count them, measure them, weigh them, analyze them. Is there any one that you would for one minute consider as over against this opportunity that Jesus was extending to these men! How you do covet that chance!

What They Were To Do The call involved a relationship. Jesus called them, Mark says, that they might be *with him*. They were not professionally-trained men. They were not especially religious men, reverent men. They had their share of all the loneliness, weakness, ignorance, and sin that normal man falls heir to on this earth. They needed to be with him for their own sakes. They needed, too, to be with him for others' sake. They could not share with others what they did not have for themselves. Of course, they would always preach more than they had experienced, for, after all, they were proclaiming the fulness of Christ and not their limited knowledge of him. Still, if they were to tell others about the Water of life, it was necessary that they should have tasted of that water. Being with him was the answer.

As difficult as it may be to believe, he chose them that *he* might be with *them*. On the human level—and remember he was man no less than God—he needed human companionship. On one occasion, he declared in prayer that no one knew him but God. He walked the earth unknown. He came unto his own and his own received him not. Later he would tell these men that they were the ones who had stood by him in his trials. He would tell them that they were not his servants but his friends. He would plead with God on the last night before he was crucified that these who had been his friends might be kept from evil and that where he was going they might one day come that they might be together forever.

Beyond companionship, he also chose them for his service. He called them that he might send them forth to do his work in his name. As Mark described it, that service would take two forms. First, he called them that he might send them forth to preach. Jesus came preaching, and he sent his disciples out to preach. God did not plan to save the world alone; he expected to have man's assistance. In Romans Paul did not understand how people could call on God if they had not believed on God, how they could believe on him if they had not heard of him, or how they were going to hear of him without a preacher. He went on to declare that God had revealed his word through preaching.

These men whom Jesus chose and sent out to preach did not forget that it was their business. On one never-to-be-forgotten day when the church was young and there were a multitude of responsibilities descending upon these men, they declared that their main business was to preach and to pray. They urged the church to assume some of the responsibility for looking after the material needs of the members;

for it was not right for the apostles to forsake the preaching of
the word of God. They had learned their lesson!

He also sent his disciples out to heal. Their first duty was
to preach the good news, but they knew that the Father was
concerned for the total person. They had watched their
Master deal gently with all the needs of men. By their own
involvement, they would reveal God's love for all men.

In *The Menninger Story,* Walker Winslow tells about the
dedication of a new hospital in Topeka, Kansas, to house the
world-famous Menninger Clinic. The old doctor who had
pioneered in the famous institution was ninety years old, and
on his birthday he was asked to lay the cornerstone for the
new hospital that was to bear his name. Outstanding citizens
from Topeka and from over the nation, as well as leading
doctors from all over the world, were present for the occasion.
When the time came for him to speak, Dr. Karl Menninger
stood; he was tall and straight; his looks belied his ninety
years. He gazed out upon the great throng of people. Later he
said that he had known at the time that the throng expected
him to give them his medical credo, and he had prepared such
a statement. When the moment came, however, he could
speak only from his heart, and this is what he said:

From the very beginning, God's hand has been guiding this,
and it is fitting to invoke His blessings on what we are going to
do. We believe that He put it into our hearts to build this hospital for the art of healing men.

After a moment of silence he bowed his head and prayed,
"Almighty God, Father of Mercies and God of all comfort, look
upon us with favor as we dedicate this building to that end.
Bless all who come here sick and troubled. And bless, we pray,
all who labor here to relieve affliction. Direct us, we beseech
Thee with thankful hearts, in Thy way of righteousness and
peace, and to Thee be glory and praise, now and forevermore.
Amen." [7]

That incident is entirely within the spirit that sent the apostles out to heal.

What They Could Expect Included within the call of Jesus was the promise of success. He said, "I will make you." He had confidence in his students to learn and confidence in himself to teach. Both were necessary. Thinking of those students as they were when Jesus called them and what they had to learn before they could measure up to his standard for them, one has a fresh view of the optimism of Jesus! It was no easy task to which he set himself, for he would accept no shortcuts in teaching and training.

In the days when men went to sea in wooden ships, an inexperienced youth visited a hiring hall in London hoping to get a job as a seaman. The first question asked was, "Have you ever gone around the Horn?" In those days shipping companies wanted experienced men, men who had made one or two trips around Cape Horn. The youth replied that he had never been around the Horn. "Then," said the agent, "you will have to come with me into the back room." There in the middle of the floor lay the horn of a steer. The agent said, "Now, young man, just walk slowly around that horn there on the floor; walk slowly." The would-be sailor did as he was instructed. "You can now qualify for the job," announced the agent. I can give you a contract to work as a seaman on a trip to India."

While Jesus would accept no shortcuts in the field of teaching and training, he did indicate to his men that former experience as fishermen would be valuable to them. He said, "I will make you fishers of men." They knew fishing of a sort, but if they would follow him, he would teach them to do some real fishing. The difference between the barefoot boy

on the bank of a lively creek catching minnows with a reed
pole and a bent pin and the skilled sportsman reeling in blue
marlin from the Gulf Stream is just a suggestion of the
difference between what they had been doing and what he
could teach them to do.

The Master never called a man to a smaller task than the
one he was originally performing. Jesus believed in promot-
ing men. It was one of the incentives that he used to get men
to leave their old jobs and accept new employment with him.
Morgan Phelps Noyes tells of a prominent woman who said
that she had done all of her work outside the church because
her church had offered her only little tasks, tasks that anyone
could perform, while other organizations in the city were
offering opportunities that demanded the great executive
abilities that she was generally recognized to possess.

There is an answer to that sort of thing. In the first place, it
is sometimes true. People are not challenged by the church. It
does not ask enough; it asks less than the world asks in time,
talents, responsibility, and sacrifice. Men and women are
challenged by big jobs. In the second place, it is entirely
possible that the woman had her scale of values all wrong,
that she did not know the difference between a big and a small
job. Some jobs that seem small are really large; some jobs
that seem large are in reality very small.

When the mother of Thomas Edison took on the teaching
of her son because the schoolteacher had said the boy was too
dull to learn, the teacher thought that the mother was wasting
her time. But the world rejoices in light today because of the
work of that mother. Even her preacher husband felt that
Susanna Wesley spent too much time with her sons, John and
Charles. To others that task seemed like a small one, and
other jobs were counted more important. It may well be that
lovingly and effectively teaching a class of boys or girls in

Sunday school is more important than guiding a great corporation.

Let it be remembered that Jesus made good his promise. He did *make* them. It took a long time; it called for great effort and patience. At times even the patience and optimism of Jesus were put to the test. On one occasion he said, and there seemed to be the ring of despair in it, "Have I been so long time with you, and yet hast thou not known." Still, they did learn; he did teach them; he did make them. Jesus satisfied their longings. There was such an authority in him that these men, used to wrestling with storms in darkness, found in him a worthier manhood. His eagerness caught their youth, his certitude their loyalty, his tenderness their love; and the divine solitude in him called to the deeps in their souls. They left home and livelihood for a life that would stretch out beyond time and place. He made them! It was not easy; at times they thought he was hard.

Years ago when a party of Arctic explorers went in search of Sir John Franklin, they encountered weather that plunged their thermometer to seventy degrees below zero. Many of the strongest men in the party began to falter. They lay down to sleep. The one in charge of the party knew that one half-hour of that treacherous sleep and the men would be stiff in death. The leader seemed cruel and brutal; he boxed their ears; he struck them; he yelled at them; he did everything possible to drive the men forward; and "the arm that roused them was the arm that saved them."

In Jesus men found courage in the place of fear, strength instead of weakness, joy instead of satiety, enthusiasm in the place of boredom, insight instead of dulness, life instead of death. Observing their behavior, the people realized "that they had been with Jesus." This small band of ignorant and unlearned men became a channel for the living water that has quenched the thirst of millions and has caused the deserts of life to blossom as the rose. No other twelve men in the history of the world have been so blessed and honored through service and sacrifice.

One final word must be said. When Christ called these men, the men still had to make a choice. He invited, he challenged, but he did not compel. He did not then; he does not now. We, too, must decide whether to follow the living Christ.

> "Fishers of men!" I can see Him stand
> Here in the boat yet. And, John, did you mind
> His voice—like the breath of the western wind,
> As He told of His Father? John, could it be
> He was speaking of God, and of you, and of me?
>
> "Fishers of men!" Is He fisherman too?
> And could we be like Him, I and you?
> John, I could follow a man such as He
> Clear through the gates of eternity.
> "Fishers of men!" If He meant me and you,
> John, let us go and be fishermen too.[8]

Notes

CHAPTER 1

1. Quoted by Leslie D. Weatherhead in *His Life and Ours* (New York: Abingdon Press, 1933), p. 73.
2. Cited by James D. Robertson in *Handbook of Preaching Resources* (New York: The Macmillan Company, 1962), p. 10.
3. Morris L. West, *The Shoes of the Fisherman* (New York: William Morrow & Co., 1963), p. 110.
4. Walter C. Smith, as quoted in Weatherhead, *op. cit.*, p. 67.
5. A. J. Gossip, "The Silent Years," *The Speaker's Bible*, ed. James Hastings (Aberdeen, Scotland: G. & W. Fraser, n.d.), St. Luke, I, 169.

CHAPTER 2

1. John Oxenham, "The Other Boys," *Christ and the Fine Arts*, Cynthia Pearl Maus, comp. (New York: Harper & Bros., 1938), p. 109.
2. *San Francisco Chronicle*, May 31, 1964, p. 1B.
3. Leslie D. Weatherhead, *How Can I Find God?* (New York: Fleming H. Revell Co., 1934), p. 126.
4. *New York Times*, Book Section, July 7, 1940, p. 19.
5. *The Autobiography of G. K. Chesterton* (New York: Sheed & Ward, 1937), p. 167.
6. G. A. Studdert-Kennedy, "The Carpenter," *Quotable Poems I*, comps., Thomas Curtis Clark and Esther A. Gillespie (Chicago: Willett, Clark and Co., 1931), p. 13.
7. G. K. Chesterton, *St. Francis of Assisi* (New York: Doubleday & Co., 1962), pp. 36–7.
8. Edwin Markham, "His Greatest Miracle," as quoted by William L. Stidger, *Planning Your Preaching* (New York: Harper & Bros., 1932), p. 71.

124 SEVEN FIRST WORDS OF JESUS

CHAPTER 3

1. From *The New Testament in Modern English,* © J. B. Phillips, 1958. Used by permission of The Macmillan Company.
2. G. A. Studdert-Kennedy, *The New Man in Christ* (London: Hodder & Stoughton, 1932), p. 194.
3. Gerald Heard, *A Dialogue in the Desert* (New York: Harper & Bros., 1942), p. 9.
4. Marc Connelly, *The Green Pastures* (New York: Rinehart & Co., 1958), pp. 25–6.
5. Henry van Dyke, "The Gospel of Labor," *Quotable Poems I,* comps., Thomas Curtis Clark and Esther A. Gillespie, *op. cit.,* p. 271.
6. Connelly, *op. cit.,* p. 105.
7. Reprinted from *The Prophet* by Kahlil Gibran with permission of the publisher, Alfred A. Knopf, Inc. Copyright 1923 by Kahlil Gibran; renewal copyright 1951 by Administrators C. T. A. of Kahlil Gibran Estate and Mary G. Gibran.
8. *San Francisco Chronicle,* February 25, 1964, p. 12.
9. As quoted by Morgan Phelps Noyes, *Preaching the Word of God* (New York: Charles Scribner's Sons, 1943), p. 118.

CHAPTER 4

1. W. J. Lederer and Eugene Burdick, *The Ugly American* (New York: W. W. Norton & Co., 1958), p. 128.
2. West, *op. cit.,* p. 231.
3. Daniel 3:16–18, *Berkeley Version of the Bible.*
4. T. S. Eliot, *The Elder Statesman* (New York: Farrar, Straus & Cudahy, 1959), p. 43.
5. Malcolm Boyd, *If I Go Down to Hell: Man's Search for Meaning in Contemporary Life* (New York: Morehouse-Barlow, 1962), p. 163.

CHAPTER 5

1. Weatherhead, *op. cit.,* p. 106.
2. Gene Smith, *When the Cheering Stopped* (New York: William Morrow & Co., 1964), p. 134.
3. Heard, *op. cit.,* p. 44.
4. *Ibid.*
5. Sylvia Thompson, *Hounds of Spring* (New York: Little, Brown & Co., 1926), p. 157.
6. Graham Greene, *The Heart of the Matter* (New York: The Viking Press, 1962), pp. 196, 203.
7. John A. T. Robinson, *Honest to God* (Philadelphia: The Westminster Press, 1963), p. 90.

8. Dorothy Parker, *Not so Deep as a Well* (New York: The Viking Press, 1955), p. 52.

9. Luke 4:18–19, RSV.

10. T. Howard Crago, *The Story of F. W. Boreham* (London: Marshall, Morgan & Scott, 1961), p. 237.

11. Vachel Lindsay, "Foreign Missions in Battle Array," *Collected Poems* (New York: The Macmillan Company, 1927), pp. 338–9.

CHAPTER 6

1. William Lyon Phelps, *Autobiography with Letters* (New York: Oxford University Press, 1939), pp. 745–6.

2. Charles Rann Kennedy, *The Terrible Meek* (New York: Samuel French, 1939), p. 39.

3. T. S. Eliot, *The Rock* (New York: Harcourt, Brace & Co., 1934), pp. 47–8.

4. Louis Untermeyer, "Caliban in the Coal Fields," *Modern American Poetry*, ed., Louis Untermeyer (New York: Harcourt, Brace & Co., 1950), p. 324.

5. West, *op. cit.,* p. 167.

6. Harry Golden, *Carl Sandburg* (Greenwich, Conn.: Fawcett Publishers, 1962), p. 168.

7. Bernard A. Weisberger, *They Gathered at the River* (Boston: Little, Brown & Co., 1958), p. 45.

CHAPTER 7

1. Theodore H. White, *The Making of the President, 1960* (New York: Atheneum Publishers, 1961).

2. Douglas Blatherwick, adapted from *The Mind of Jesus,* William Barclay (New York: Harper and Bros., 1961), p. 61.

3. Elizabeth O'Conner, *Call to Commitment* (New York: Harper & Row, 1963), p. 39.

4. Walter Russell Bowie, *The Master, A Life of Jesus Christ* (New York: Charles Scribner's Sons, 1928), p. 101.

5. James S. Stewart, *The Life and Teaching of Jesus Christ* (Edinburgh: Church of Scotland Committee on Youth, 1934), p. 62.

6. Mark 1:16–20, RSV.

7. Walker Winslow, *The Menninger Story* (Garden City: Doubleday & Co., 1956), p. 24.

8. Quoted in *The Speaker's Bible,* ed., James Hastings, Mark, I, 27.